I0820453

Mandi Em

Celia Agnes

# That Crystal Vibe

H

Dedicated to my children—Dominic, Noah, and Natalie—who fill my life with magic, joy and positive energy.—M. E.

To my husband, Josh, for being a relentless encouragement and wonderful provider, and believing in my art from the very beginning.—C. A.

First published in 2026 by Holler, an imprint of The Quarto Group.
100 Cummings Center, Suite 265D, Beverly, MA 01915, USA.
T +1 978-282-9590
**www.Quarto.com**

EEA Representation, WTS Tax d.o.o., Žanova ulica 3, 4000 Kranj, Slovenia.
www.wts-tax.si



ISBN 978-0-7112-9786-9
EBook ISBN 978-0-7112-9787-6

Designer: Michelle Brackenborough
In-house Design: Lyli Feng
Commissioning Editor: Alex Hithersay
Production Controller: Nikki Ingram
Art Director: Karissa Santos
Publisher: Debbie Foy

Manufactured in Guangdong, China TT112025

9 8 7 6 5 4 3 2 1

The paper and board used in this book are made from wood from responsible sources.

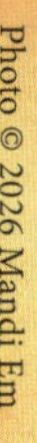
Photo © 2026 Mandi Em

## About the author

**Mandi Em** is a humorist, author, and psychospiritual guide who makes spiritual self-care simple, fun, and accessible. She's the author of *Witchcraft Therapy*, *Happy Witch*, *Feral Self-Care*, and *Shadow Work for Hot Messes*, and the creator behind *Healing for Hot Messes*. Through her books, programs, and intuitive energy readings, she helps people ditch self-help misery mode and find playful, practical ways to reprogram their reality. Her work has been featured in *The New York Times*, *HuffPost*, *Refinery29*, *SheKnows*, *McSweeneys*, and more. She and her husband are born-again hippies raising their three children in beautiful Vernon, British Columbia.

# Contents

**Welcome** 7
*How to Use This Book* 8

PART I: **Rock Your Wellness:** *An introduction to crystal healing*

**What Are Crystals and Why Are They Special?** 13
*How Crystals Form in Nature* 16
*The Rise of Lab-Grown Crystals* 18
*Scientific and Practical Applications* 19

**Why Crystals for Wellness?** 22
*Crystal Healing Through History* 23
*Mindset and Worldview* 25

**Crystals and Energy Healing** 28

**Ethics of Crystal Healing** 30

PART II: **Know Your Stones:** *Ethical sourcing and connecting with your collection*

**Sourcing Your Crystals** 35
*How to Use Your Intuition When Selecting Crystals* 36

**Ethical Sourcing** 37

**Crystals Versus Rocks** 39

**Types and Shapes of Crystals** 41

**Safety Considerations** 45
*Safety First* 45
*Crystal Never-Evers* 47

**Crystal Care and Storage** 48

**Cleansing and Charging Your Crystals** 51

PART III: **Prismatic Wellness:** *Getting started using crystals as a tool for mindfulness and self-care*

**Crystals and Correspondences** 57

**Programming Your Crystals** 60

**Crystals in the Home** 62

**Crystals and Sacred Geometry** 66
*Using Crystal Grids* 67

**Crystals and Energetic Grounding** 69

**Crystals and Setting Up Sacred Space** 71

**Wearing Crystals** 73

**Bathing with Crystals** 76

**Crystals and Divination** 78

**Crystals and Sound Healing** 80

**Crystals and Astrology** 82
*The Zodiac Signs and Their Common Characteristics* 83

**Crystals and Tarot** 85
*Using Crystals to Enhance Your Tarot Practice* 86

**Crystals to Charge Other Items** 88

PART IV: **Crystalline Counsel:** *Stones and practices to troubleshoot hard times*

**Crystals and Anxiety** 93

**Crystals and Protection** 97

**Crystals and Depression** 101

**Crystals and Experiencing Loss** 105

**Crystals for Calm** 109

**Crystals for Self-Love and Acceptance** 113

**Crystals and Confidence** 117

**Crystals for Empowered Self Expression** 121

**Crystals and Creativity** 125

**Crystals for Energy** 129

**Crystals and Connecting to Intuition and the Higher Self** 133

**Crystals for Abundance** 137

**Your Crystal Care Plan** 141

*Glossary* 144

# Welcome

Crystals have been a source of fascination for humans through the ages. Whether it be the multifaceted sparkling of an aura quartz cluster or the natural rocky surface of an unpolished howlite, these stones dazzled and amazed our species long before we understood how extraordinary they are on a molecular level. There is something about these unique and beautiful stones that has captured the human imagination, and made them a staple for ritual, healing, and aesthetic purposes, throughout our history.

Many of the crystals we know and love were formed deep in the earth through natural processes. They are treasures of Mother Nature that illustrate the wonders of the science that governs this planet and the beauty found in the chaos of nature. Working with crystals to enhance your mindfulness and self-care routines is a fun and vibey way to invite these treasures into your life. These stones are not only pleasing to the eye, but also have a long history of spiritual use, being seen as sacred tools for amplifying and transmuting energies. Crystals have a variety of everyday uses in the modern age as well, solidifying their importance and value to our species.

When reflecting on my own introduction to crystals, I uncovered a collection of memories that you may find relatable. Finding glittering stones as a child and filling my pockets with only the most special ones. Being in mysteriously scented bookshops and gift shops alongside my mother, with large geodes, globes, and prisms lining the shelves and windows. I recall the rock tumbler I got as a gift one year, and the excitement of waiting to see what result I would get when tossing in the various rocks I had collected. Although these were not all encounters with true crystals, they were my initiations into the beauty and spectacle of nature. As I grew older, crystals became items to marvel at and yearn for, but it wasn't until I opened to the world of energies, frequency, and vibration that I fully got to experience their power.

In this book, you will learn the basics of crystals and energy healing, and get advice for using them as part of your self-care practices to troubleshoot specific, common issues causing drama and disruptions in your peace. If you've been wondering how to begin collecting and connecting with your crystals, *That Crystal Vibe* is for you! Within these pages we will dive into the crystal conversation and explore how these stones can be used in tandem with tarot, astrology, divination, and more.

*Before we dive in, ask yourself:*

*What drew you to crystal healing?*

*What are your motivations, curiosities, and intentions for your budding interest in crystals?*

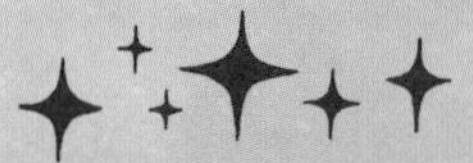

## How to Use This Book

*That Crystal Vibe* is your fun and handy introduction to the world of crystal healing!

Specifically, this book will help you:

- *Gain a foundational understanding of crystals and healing stones*
- *Get started with practical advice on how to source your collection in an ethical manner*
- *Learn how to incorporate crystals into your wellness practices, both alone and combined with other modalities*
- *Learn actionable methods for using crystals to tackle specific wellness woes*

While crystals are a beautiful and enjoyable way to incorporate some of Mother Nature's magic into your world, it's important to note that these are fun and fascinating *additions* to your self-care and healing efforts. Make sure that you seek medical or professional help when needed, as crystals are in no way a replacement for doctors or other forms of medical and mental health care. Don't get it twisted—there's a great deal of power in working with crystals and other stones; however, they are not always the best tool for the job. Think critically about any metaphysical wellness claims that may come up in the crystal conversation, whether it be in books, online, or in person. This isn't to discount crystal or energy healing, but simply a warning to tread cautiously when big claims are made that may leave you or somebody else unsafe or vulnerable.

As you move through this book, pay keen attention to the sections on ethical sourcing and safety to ensure that you get the most from your crystal practices. Learning about some of the ethical concerns around sourcing crystals will help you ensure that your collection is considerately compiled rather than contributing to the capitalist destruction that's been a byproduct of the rising demand for these stones. The safety considerations will ensure not only that you keep your crystals safe, but that you keep yourself safe too.

Throughout this book there will be diagrams, prompts, and more to help you get the most out of the information presented. Working with crystals is a hands-on practice. One of the greatest things about crystal healing is that it empowers you to tap into your own intuition and creativity, and this can start right here, right now, as you learn!

PART I

# Rock Your Wellness

## An introduction to crystal healing

# What Are Crystals and Why Are They Special?

Humans have revered crystals and utilized them for sacred and ritual purposes since ancient times. Long before we had online markets and lab-grown crystals, we recognized these remarkable stones for their beauty, symmetry, and energetic power. Throughout history, we have used them for healing, connecting to spirit, decor and adornment, and shifting and transmuting energies.

## *But what are crystals, and why are they considered special?*

Crystals earn their classification as "crystalline solids" based on their unique molecular structure. Technically, crystals are set apart from other stones as, at the molecular level, they have a highly organized, three-dimensional structure, which allows them to vibrate and energetically operate in a distinct manner. The molecular structure of crystals is geometrically perfect, repetitive, and forms a grid-like pattern.

Despite these technical definitions of what constitutes a crystal, a variety of other stones are often included in the crystal conversation. Obsidian, a type of volcanic glass, is one example of an "amorphous" stone that is grouped with crystals and has a rich history of sacred use by humans.

## Crystals, Minerals, Gemstones, or Rocks?

*We've talked about the definition of crystals but where do minerals, gemstones, and rocks factor in?*

***Minerals*** *are defined as structures that are natural and inorganic, typically with a crystalline structure.*

***Gemstones*** *are rare precious or semi-precious stones, classified based on their value.*

***Rocks*** *are naturally occurring stones that contain aggregates of various minerals and sometimes also organic material.*

***Amorphous crystals*** *do not fit the typical definition of crystals, as they do not feature highly organized repetitive patterns on the micro-scale. They include amber, a resinous stone, and moldavite, a tektite formed from meteorite impact.*

When it comes to crystal healing, the type of stone used and how and where it was formed are all taken into consideration. Some people believe that the way a crystal develops contributes to its properties or correspondences. One of my own favorite stones for strength is a piece of lava rock I was sent from an active eruption in Iceland. The energy from this stone is palpable—carried forward from its inception under intense heat and pressure. This is my go-to stone for motivation, power, and the strength to go with the flow in times of chaos!

Crystal healing is all about energetics and vibration, concepts we will get into more in Part IV.

Essentially, due to the unique structure of crystals, they are approached as sacred tools that can shift the vibrations and frequencies of people, environments, and objects. Some even consider crystals a type of entity or lifeform.

Different stones are considered to have different uses, meanings, and correspondences. For instance:

- *Some stones are considered* ***amplifiers****, which means they are meant to* raise *or* boost *energies.*
- *Some stones are considered* ***transmuters****, which means they are meant to* transform *or* change *energies.*
- *Some stones are considered* ***cleansers****, which means they are used to* clear *or* absorb *negative or unwanted energies.*
- *Some stones are considered* ***attractors****, shaking up the status quo and* drawing in *certain things or circumstances.*

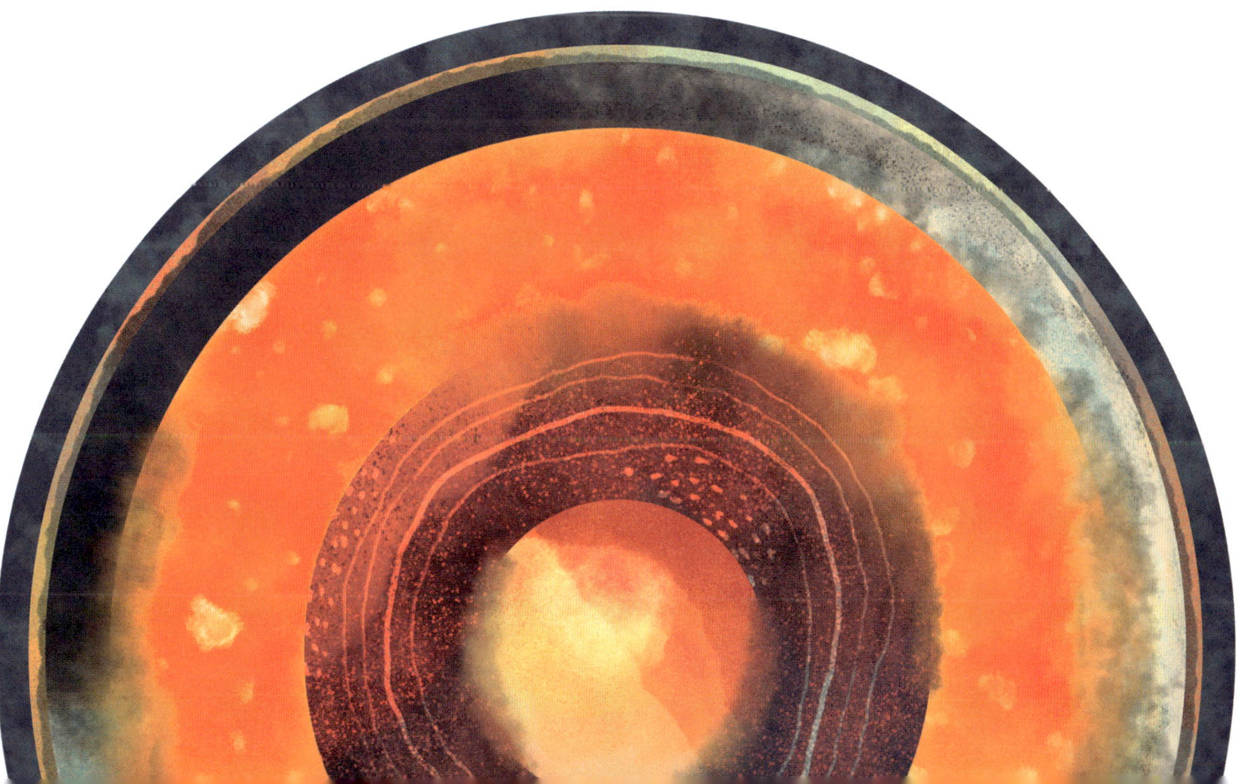

# How Crystals Form in Nature

Crystals typically form over time in wildly intense conditions. They are dazzling works of the science and artistry of Earth's natural geological processes.

Crystals form in a variety of ways, which can affect their structure and appearance. Some contributing factors that play a role in crystal formation—also known as *crystallization*—include:

- *Intense pressure*
- *High temperatures*
- *Rapid or slow cooldown periods*
- *Layering of moisture and minerals*
- *Water or moisture evaporation*

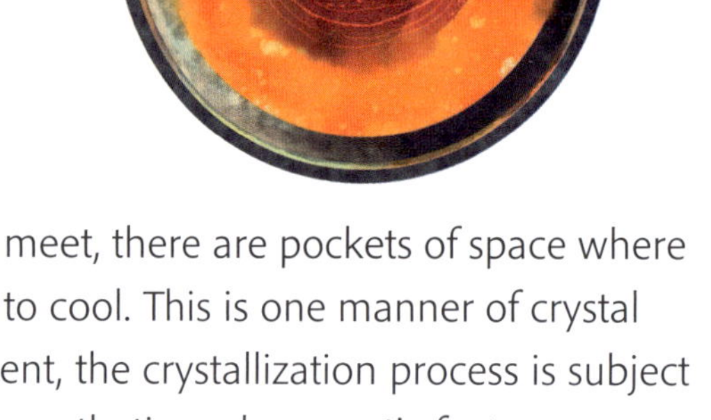

For instance, where Earth's crust and mantle meet, there are pockets of space where molten rock (or magma) collects and begins to cool. This is one manner of crystal formation. In this chaotic, dynamic environment, the crystallization process is subject to changing conditions, and some interesting aesthetic and energetic features can take shape within these stones.

Let's revisit the definition of a crystal. Crystals are solid substances in which the atoms, molecules, or ions are arranged in an extremely organized and repetitive geometric pattern known as a crystal lattice. Sometimes, the faces of these stones may reflect the geometry and symmetry that are present internally, causing the crystal to have unique shapes, facets, and layers.

Crystallography is the study of crystallization. Crystallization is not a process that occurs only in stones. Water freezing into ice is also a kind of crystallization. Salt and sugar are both examples of crystals you can find around the house.

# Crystal Lattice Patterns

*There are seven molecular crystal lattice patterns seen in crystallography*

| PATTERN | INNER STRUCTURE | EXAMPLE CRYSTAL |
|---|---|---|
| Cubic | Square | Fluorite |
| Triclinic | Three inclined angles | Labradorite |
| Monoclinic | Parallelogram | Moonstone |
| Orthorhombic | Diamond-shaped | Celestite |
| Tetragonal | Rectangular | Scapolite |
| Trigonal | Triangular | Citrine |
| Hexagonal | Hexagonal | Aquamarine |

It's important to note that not all crystals are safe to use, ingest, or handle. Asbestos is an example of a crystalline material that you definitely **wouldn't want** to tuck in your pocket or make an elixir from! Make sure you read the sections on safety in this book, and commit to ongoing learning when it comes to crystal safety. Sadly, there is far too much incomplete or misleading information out there, so it's important to stay safe.

## Did you know?

*Crystals can form in the bodies of some animals! Kidney stones are one example of mineral crystallization that occurs within the body.*

## The Rise of Lab-Grown Crystals

We are now capable of growing synthetic crystals that are chemically and structurally the same as naturally occurring crystals. These *are* real crystals; however, they are intentionally formed in controlled conditions rather than being gifts from nature. There is some debate about the energetics of synthetic crystals, but given the moral concerns associated with the demand for stones, some consider synthetic crystals to be a more sustainable alternative. We will talk more about the ethics of lab-grown crystals in the section on ethical sourcing (page 37).

As we saw with the example of obsidian earlier, some stones that are commonly grouped with crystals do not seem to fit when it comes to the scientific definition. These are known as amorphous crystals, and although they may have a long history of sacred use and be commonly recommended for inclusion in your crystal collection, they *do not* fit the scientific criteria for crystal designation. Since using crystals for healing and energetics is different from the scientific study of crystallography or geology, the word "crystal" gets more of a broad treatment when talking about spiritual uses.

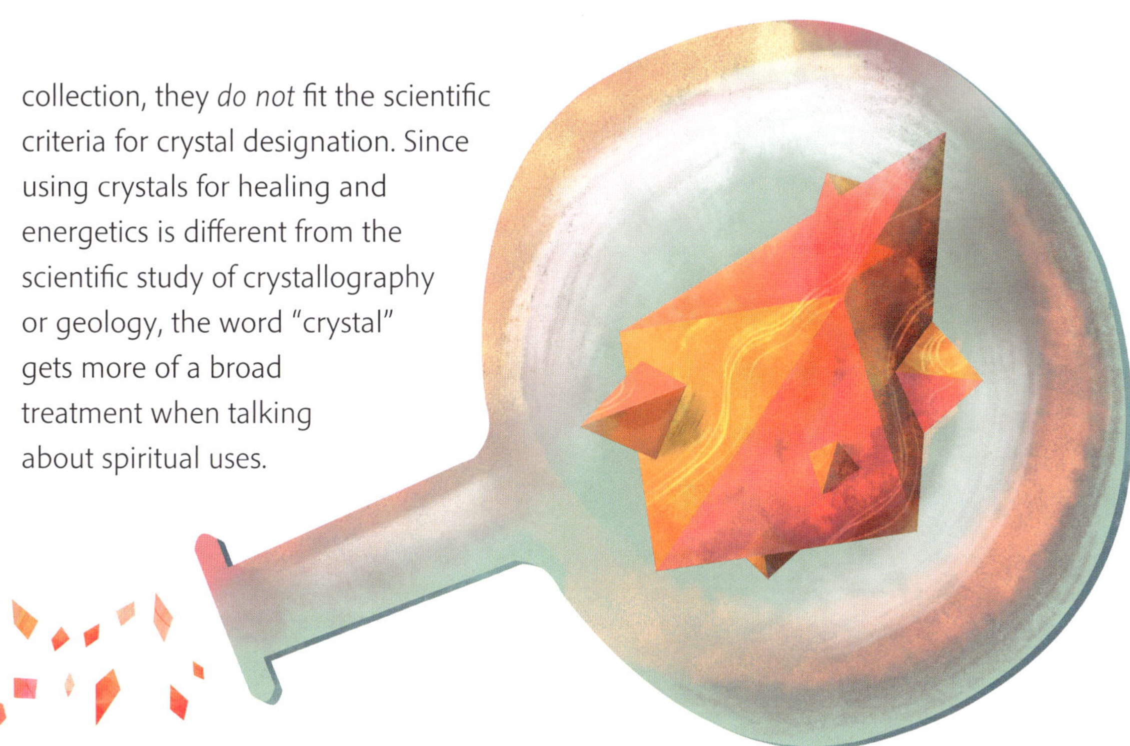

## Scientific and Practical Applications

Fascination with crystals has endured from ancient times into modernity, with crystals acting as key players in some spiritual and New Age movements, which use them as energetic tools for healing, manifesting, and more. But crystals don't just grace the shelves of metaphysical shops and the pockets of pagans. They are all around us, used in a variety of household and practical applications.

Some examples of crystals in practical applications you can find around the home include:

- *Pencils containing graphite*
- *A diamond wedding ring*
- *A quartz timepiece, such as a watch*
- *Computer processors and other technologies containing quartz*

## Piezoelectricity and Pyroelectricity

*No conversation about the science of crystals would be complete without mentioning the **piezoelectric** effect, which is often cited by crystal enthusiasts as evidence of their electric and energetic power. This is when an electrical effect, or voltage, is created by applying mechanical pressure to certain crystals (such as quartz). To put it simply, when a quartz or other piezoelectric crystal is stressed under pressure, it creates an electrical charge, much like a battery. The reverse piezoelectric effect is when electricity is run through one of these crystals and it vibrates to adjust, causing it to conduct electricity.*

*Another notable property that certain crystals have is **pyroelectricity**. This is the ability for some crystals to create electrical voltage when heated or cooled. The change in temperature can cause the molecules to shift and change polarization, creating an electric field.*

A quartz watch is a good example of crystal use in a regular household item. Due to its piezoelectric properties and precise vibrational frequency, using quartz in a timepiece ensures that the time kept is about as accurate as it's possible to get.

Crystalline elements are also found in a variety of other technologies. For example, silicon, a component in many electronic devices (such as computer processors), is derived from quartz. Crystals have long been used for sonar, radio, and more. Again, it is their unique and highly ordered internal structure that means they are vibrationally stable enough to make them an asset in various technologies.

Now, these aren't in the same form as the crystals we use for mindfulness practices. In these applications, crystal elements or derivatives are used as components, and we likely wouldn't recognize them as crystals like we do a glittering geode, tower, or palmstone!

It's important to know about these practical applications of crystals because they highlight just how special crystals are. Those who dismiss crystal healing often refer to them as "just rocks." While it's one thing not to vibe with the concepts of energy, frequency, and vibrational healing and wellness, it's another to call crystals "just rocks." The reality is these stones are structurally and energetically unique and notable. They are marvels of nature—and should be appreciated and recognized as such.

Crystals were used and valued for their unique properties even before our species had the scientific tools to understand their underlying structure. Perhaps it is possible that our ancestors had some knowledge that we in the modern era still do not possess.

# Why Crystals for Wellness?

***Crystals are accessible*** For the most part, crystal healing is a DIY endeavor that is intuitive and customizable, and which you can do at your own pace. There are no appointments to go to, no strict "rules," and you can work with crystals in either simple or elaborate ways. For some, a crystal practice is as casual as wearing the stones as jewelry or carrying them in their pockets; while for others, crystals may be used in rituals and scattered throughout the home to direct energies. There are best practices when working with crystals, but overall, cultivating a relationship with them is something you can do at any age, at any time of day, and that can evolve with you over time.

***Crystals allow us to connect with our primal ancestry***
Crystals have been used for spiritual and wellness purposes for millennia, so working with them in the modern context lets us tap into a primal part of our humanity. A hallmark of the modern era is full dismissal of anything that we cannot prove using the scientific method. This is a good thing in many ways, but we as a species have lost touch with the mysteries along the way. We tend to deem our ancient ancestors lacking in knowledge and understanding, and this may not be the right attitude to take. Many people view energy medicine as the next frontier of wellness, and we might need to look at a revival of ancient practices with openness and humility.

## Crystals allow us to connect with and appreciate nature

Our species is in dire need of a wake-up call when it comes to how we connect and interact with nature. After many years of dominating and polluting the planet, we could use a serious return to our roots: recognizing ourselves as a part of nature, rather than separate from it. The more we learn about and work with crystals, the more we may begin to appreciate the beauty and artistry of the natural world. The essence of crystal healing is a belief that these stones help us to align and focus energies, that they are treasures of the earth that have a vibrational and energetic effect on us and our environments. For some, this may be a gateway to understanding that we can have a dynamic and fulfilling relationship with Mother Nature and her gifts.

# Crystal Healing Through History

References to crystal healing have been found throughout the world, going back to the earliest manifestations of human civilization. There are references to crystals being used as metaphysical tools in the early civilizations of Egypt, South America, India, China, Mesopotamia, Greece, and many others all over the world. The use of crystals for healing, energy, and spiritual wellness has cut across cultures and time. It is deeply entwined with our evolution as a species.

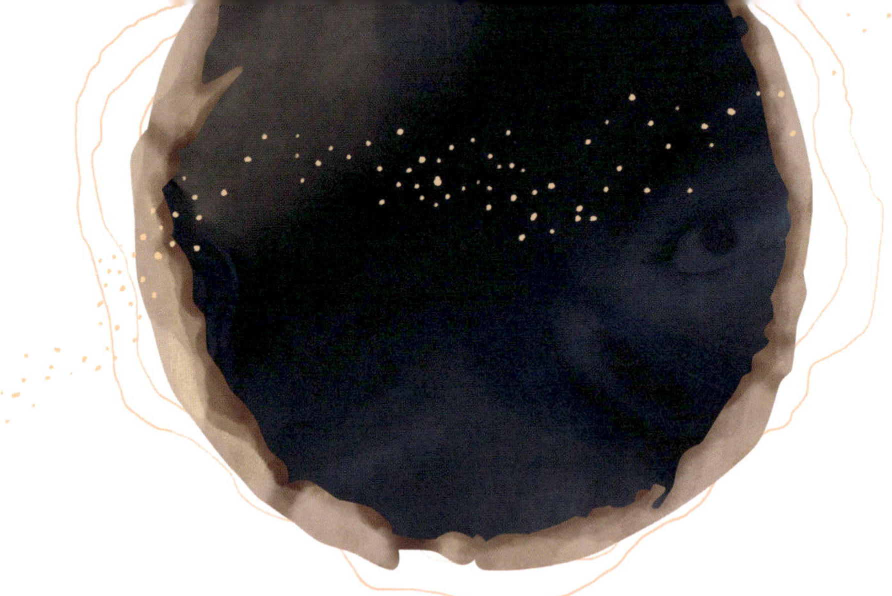

## Obsidian Mirrors

*The oldest mirrors we have found were made of obsidian and discovered at the Neolithic site of Çatalhöyük in Turkey. Obsidian mirrors have been used throughout history for various ritual and ceremonial purposes, such as scrying (a method of divination).*

## Shamanism

*Shamanism is considered one of the world's oldest belief sytems. Although the word "shaman" comes from the medicine people of Siberia and Eastern Europe, it has evolved to be a working definition of the medicine people, healers, and go-betweens of the earthly and spirit realms across cultures. In many ancient and indigenous societies, crystals were and continue to be sacred tools for the shaman to connect with the spirit realm and transmute energies. Shamanic practices that use crystals include the removal of malicious entities, turning one type of energy to another, harnessing protective stones for guidance and spiritual safety, and many others.*

Throughout history, crystals have been associated with specific deities or other supernatural entities and have influenced myth and culture. Crystals would sometimes act as stand-ins for certain qualities of these deities, lending power or specific attributes to the person who wore them. The Vedas, sacred texts of Hinduism, describe how crystals originated from the demise of an entity, with each type of crystal corresponding to certain body parts or functions. In Egypt, particular stones were associated with gods and worn for protection and adornment, and have been found in burial sites.

In many cases, the modern use of crystals in New Age, pagan, and spiritual circles has been influenced greatly by the correspondences and practices of ancient peoples—for example, the astrological correspondences of stones, the correspondences of certain stones with the chakra system, and the association of certain stones with specific areas or functions of the body.

There have also been times when the use of crystals has fallen out of favor. Even today, crystal healing and other forms of complementary energy medicine are often dismissed due to a lack of scientific evidence. There are many things we still do not understand, and as long as we are not using *only* crystals to deal with medical issues, there is no harm in exploring crystals as a wellness tool and forming our own experiential conclusions.

## Mindset and Worldview

What you get from your relationships with your crystals depends on your approach to them. This requires taking a look at your mindset, worldview, and beliefs when it comes to crystals and energy healing.

Using crystal healing as a mindfulness tool or form of self-care starts with an openness to the idea of energetics in the esoteric (meaning hidden or unseen) sense. The idea of energetics in this context is that living things have an energetic "field" that can interact with and be influenced by the environment, objects, other creatures, etc. Like everything, we are composed of molecules that vibrate, emitting electromagnetic waves. Although it's easy to look at your human body and see it as a solid mass of YOU, on a particle level, things become a little less clearly defined and stable.

The fundamental idea of energy medicine (of which crystals are but one modality) is that our bodies emit a field of energy that is influenced by a variety of internal and external factors. Internal factors may include physical or mental illness or imbalance, stress, and overstimulation, and even our thoughts and emotions. When you hear talk about "vibrational frequencies" in this context, it is the idea that the vibration of a person's energy field is emitting a certain energetic signature, or frequency, and that this frequency may affect their emotional and physical health.

Proponents of crystal healing often believe crystals can realign or transmute (transform or change) energies in our field. This is one example of our field being influenced by external energies or factors. Part of this belief is the understanding that crystals themselves are emitting a field of energy that can interact with our own. Energy medicine ideals typically view other objects and even places as having their own energetic characteristics as well. The worldview in energy healing is that all things are in some way "alive," and that we are all part of a dynamic system of vibrational interaction and influence.

> ***"In a crystal we have clear evidence of the existence of a formative life principle, and though we cannot understand the life of a crystal, it is nonetheless a living being."*** *— Nikola Tesla*

To begin to understand your own mindset when it comes to crystals, ask yourself:

- *What feels true and possible to you?*
- *Does the concept of energy healing feel compelling to you?*
- *Do you feel anything in your body while holding or looking at crystals?*

- *Do you think that crystals can be useful as a tool for supplemental healing?*
- *Have you ever experienced something that defied scientific or logical explanation?*
- *Is there any part of you that is sceptical, and if so, are you able to find a way around it to work with these stones?*

Under the modern worldview of scientific rationalism, crystal and energy healing is largely dismissed as a pseudoscience that is only as relevant as a person's belief in it. This may be a practical viewpoint, but it also may be too quick to reject something we don't yet fully understand.

The interaction of mind and body continues to be a source of inquiry and fascination. Many of us who work with crystals do not believe that their influence is strictly the placebo effect. The fact that these stones were revered long before we knew their unique properties on a molecular level may just be evidence that their importance to our species goes beyond what we've been able to test through the lens of modern science.

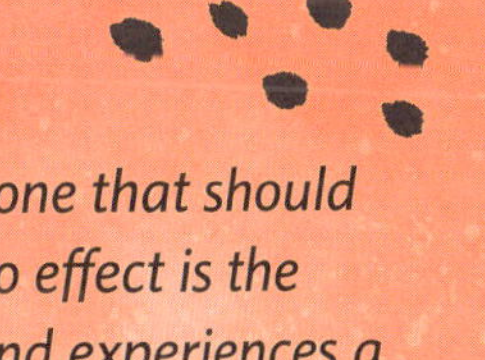

## The Placebo Effect

*A placebo is a "dummy" remedy: an intervention given to someone that should have no real measurable effect on their condition. The placebo effect is the phenomenon where a sick person is given a placebo treatment and experiences a healing effect despite the remedy being "inactive." Typically, a placebo treatment is given to a person without their knowledge. As if this effect isn't a strong enough example of mind over matter, get this: studies show there can still be a placebo effect even when a person knows they are receiving an inactive treatment!*

The most important thing is to remain open-minded and to begin forming your own ideas and beliefs based on your experiences. Just stay grounded, make sure you are keeping yourself safe and looked-after, and move from there.

# Crystals and Energy Healing

The basis of crystal healing is **energy healing**. Energy healing is based on the concept that there are subtle energies all around us, including in and surrounding our own bodies, and that all living things have specific energetic properties. Building on this, the idea is that we can work with these energies to improve our wellness or circumstances.

When you are feeling sad, or when you are excited, in love, happy, or scared, try to notice how the emotion manifests in your energy. If you have ever wondered how you can perceive this energy, consider how it feels when you go to a location that has a heavy history, or when you walk into a room where you have been the topic of discussion! Most of us have experienced subtle energies in a variety of ways, while also taking these experiences completely for granted.

Although science has still not found conclusive evidence for this kind of energy, it is known that the human body has an electromagnetic field. And many of us have experienced shifts in our energy or field. The enduring idea throughout history of crystals being intertwined with human healing and energetics gives us a clue that there may be something at play that our ancestors were more open to.

Again, when it comes to crystal healing, it's important to stay grounded and recognize that crystals as we know and work with them cannot cure all that ails us. A tricky ethical issue pops up with claims like this. Crystals can be a wonderful form of supplemental care but should not be approached as the magic cure to all illnesses. Medical science exists for a reason, and that reason is to keep us safe. However, just as someone may use a prayer or set an intention for healing, crystals can be a wonderful addendum to your treatment plan.

It is advised to connect with the energy of your crystals by holding one in your hand, then taking a deep breath, clearing your mind, and paying keen attention to what you feel and where you feel it. Some people find that they feel a zap, change in temperature, or other somatic shifts. How does the crystal make you feel and where do you feel it?

Crystals have often been connected to certain body parts, energy centers, and moods. Popular energy healing modalities, such as reiki, will often use crystals as a part of treatment. These can be placed on the body in specific areas to clear blockages, improve energy flow, and lend a little boost of whatever's needed to balance energies.

# Ethics of Crystal Healing

Although using crystals for mindfulness and self-care can be a beautiful and healing practice, there are some ethical issues that plague the crystal conversation. Here are some ethical considerations to bear in mind when starting out on your crystal journey:

*Beware of lofty claims!* Be wary of any pseudoscientific claims that try to pose these supplementary tools as the only avenue to healing. It is highly unethical for people to make these sorts of claims, which can put others at risk if taken at face value. It is dangerous not to seek the proper care for yourself if you are in a vulnerable situation. There is no reason to put off getting medical or mental health help, even if you are a huge advocate for crystals as a healing modality. Keep yourself safe!

*Environmental impacts of crystal mining* In some areas of the world, meeting the demand of the crystal craze can result in habitat loss for animals, ecosystem disruption for plants and insects, and pollution. There may also be ethical concerns when it comes to the resources needed for lab-grown crystals. In the section on ethical sourcing, page 37, you will find more information on how to obtain your crystals in a sustainable manner.

*Human rights abuses and issues* In some areas of the world, crystal mining may impact the people of the region in a negative way. The working conditions, wages, and safety of those working to supply crystals to the market can be rife with human rights abuses. There are also some regions where these resources may be controlled by or funding groups that have dire consequences for the local people. Again, more tips will be given on how to source your crystals in the section on ethical sourcing.

*Beware of counterfeit stones!* Any time a resource is in demand, there is potential for fakery! When suppliers are not careful to consider the ethical sourcing of crystals, they may (intentionally or unintentionally) sell counterfeit stones. This is an ethical issue, since we, the consumers, end up getting duped.

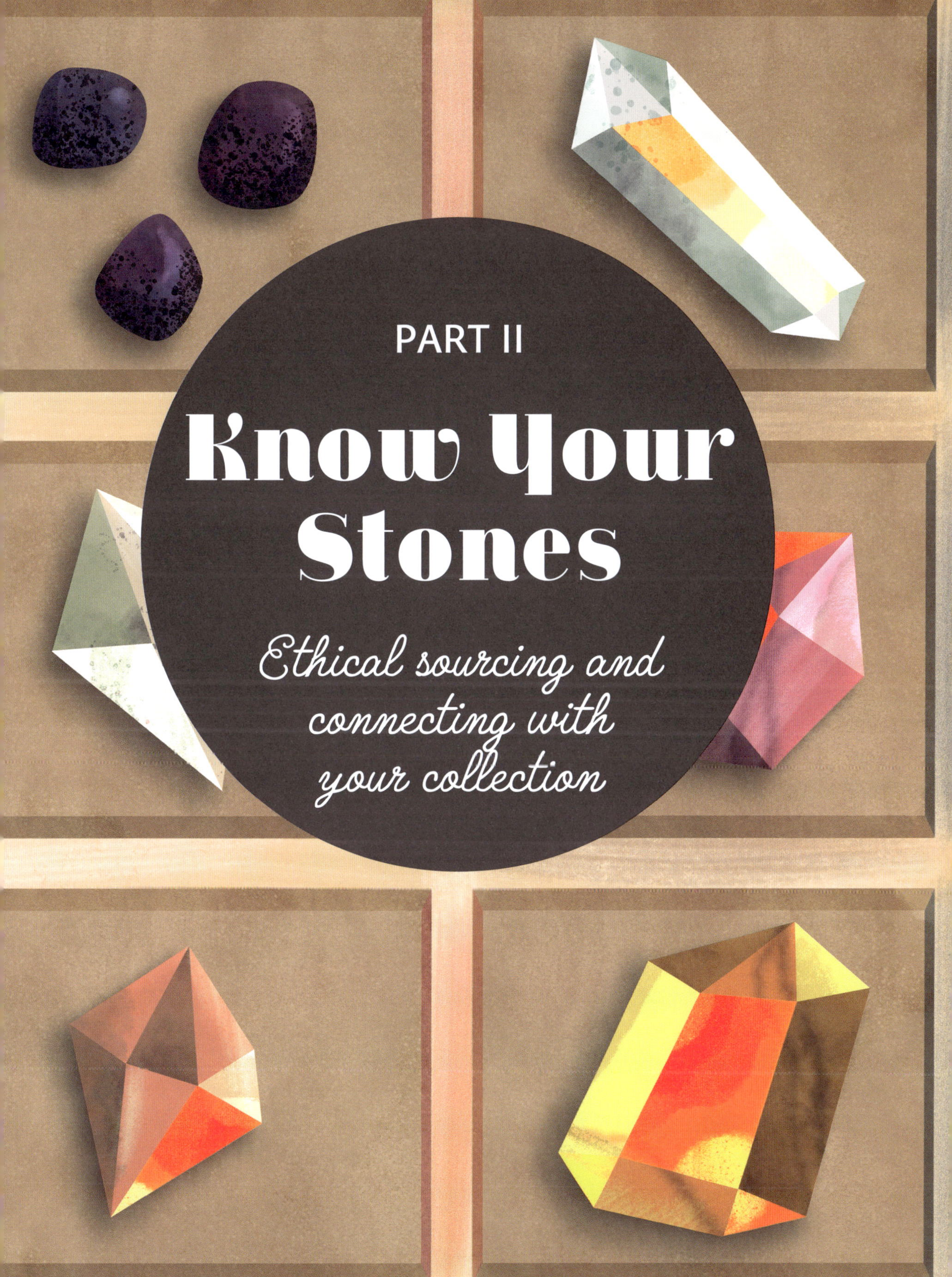
PART II
Know Your Stones
Ethical sourcing and connecting with your collection

# Sourcing Your Crystals

The following are a few ways to source crystals for your budding collection:

- *Crystals can be found in a variety of places, including the great outdoors. You can join a local lapidary club to learn more about stones and stone collecting (although attitudes toward crystal healing as a concept may vary). In some regions, it is possible to hunt for geodes or other crystals, minerals, and gems. However, be warned: rock hounds may not be so keen to share their spots with others, or spaces may already be "claimed!"*

- *In some areas you may have access to crystal and gem shows. These are events where vendors come together (like a convention) and showcase their wares. At these shows you can often find a variety of crystals, crystal jewelry or decor, and more.*

- *At local metaphysical or crystal shops, you can often have a conversation about how and where their stones were sourced. This not only helps you make connections within your own community, but may give you peace of mind when it comes to the kind of energetics you are bringing into your life. Another bonus is that you will usually be able to see and handle the stones, which allows you to listen to your intuition or see which of these crystals chooses you.*

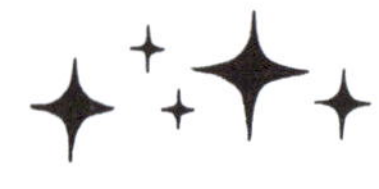

# How to Use Your Intuition When Selecting Crystals

Some people believe that the crystals you need will come to you! When choosing a crystal, try to connect with your intuition to make the right choice. In a store where you can see and handle the stones, this can be as simple as holding a stone and getting a read on whether it gives you any specific feelings or physical sensations.

Some people find that they feel an electric charge from a crystal, a change in temperature, or a buzzing sensation. Every person has a different intuitive "language." For some, this can be hearing an inner voice, sensing a certain feeling in the body—a gut feeling—or any number of other responses that indicate their intuition is speaking to them.

# Ethical Sourcing

If you want your collection to have truly good vibes, it's vital to consider ethically sourcing your crystals. How positive is the energy of your crystal going to be if it was mined in conditions that were detrimental to people or the environment? These factors should be on your radar when sourcing crystals, particularly if you are using them to enhance your wellness and mindset. Objects can collect the frequencies and vibrations of the energetic environments in which they are prepared.

There are a variety of ways to obtain crystals ethically. It takes research, but when you build your crystal collection in an ethical, intentional way, your practices will be enhanced with positive energy. As a side benefit, you are more likely to find genuine crystals when you are sourcing from a shop that truly knows their stones and where they came from. Crystals are so popular that there are a lot of fakes and stones with no discernible history out there. In general, it is better to source from merchants who not only know and understand crystals (including crystal healing, how and where they are mined, and how to care for them) but who also communicate these things to the consumer.

When you find a shop or supplier that you are thinking of purchasing from, you can do your due diligence by asking where and how their stones were mined. Pay attention to the depth of their answer. In many cases, shops may not have done their research into the conditions that led to their supply. This is especially true with large retailers or corporations that may only be trying to capitalize on the crystal craze.

The ethical concerns of the demand for crystals have been well documented, and there has been a rise in suppliers whose intention is to meet the demand for ethically sourced stones. You can find these retailers online, at crystal and gem shows, and—if you're lucky—locally. These suppliers have taken a stand against some of the unsavory practices in the crystal industry, and they will likely be more than happy to fill you in on the history of their stock. However, do not rely on just their word that they ethically source their crystals; many companies can be less than honest in their marketing. That being said, a huge green flag for finding truly ethical shops is the level of knowledge and information they will have about where their crystals come from and the lives of those who are involved in their extraction.

We've already noted the existence of synthetic or lab-grown crystals. Some claim these are an ethical way to meet the demands of the crystal market—but this is not always the case! The companies, processes, and resource needs of the lab-grown crystal industry can all have their issues as well. The important thing as a consumer is to do your research and communicate with sellers about the history of their stock.

## Ethical Crystals Wanted!

Here are some good examples of questions to get you started when sourcing your stones:

- *What region were these crystals sourced from?*
- *Does the seller know the movements of the crystals between being mined and landing in their shop?*
- *Do they know anything about the method by which these stones were mined or the working conditions of the people who collected them?*
- *Were these lab-produced crystals?*

# Crystals Versus Rocks

Although crystals are special on both an energetic and a molecular level, there is something to be said about rocks you find in nature that simply call to you. There is a reason that we as children eagerly gather these in our pockets—a habit that, for some of us, continues into adulthood!

Many rocks contain crystalline minerals, even if they are simply "rocks" by classification. Although their potency and power may be different to a crystal's, I would urge you to listen to your spirit when you are out in nature and a stone calls to you. There is energy all around us in the natural world, and when you connect with something there is value in that. Consider this: which stone may end up being more powerful for you? A rock that spoke to you on a day or in a location of great importance, or an actual crystal that you purchased online, sight unseen? Although they may both have power, the significance of the rock you found should not be understated!

We humans have a tendency to gather and collect things. Sometimes we are attracted to stones based on their shape, color, location, time of finding, or simply the feeling they bring out in us. To indulge this form of playful interaction with the natural world is a beautiful thing.

The crystal healing conversation, at its core, is about intangible associations. It's about intention and the fluid nature of the subtle energy body. For this reason, we should not shy away from paying attention to the importance of what our emotions, spirit, and senses tell us about objects, particularly in the natural world, where everything feels as if it is brimming with life.

# Types and Shapes of Crystals

When it comes to considering a crystal's shape, you should begin by thinking about your intention for the crystal. Are you looking for something to use to influence or direct the energy in your home? Something to meditate or do grounding exercises with? Something for targeted energy direction? Something that is easy to hold? To wear?

Some considerations when choosing crystal shapes:

- *The directionality of the surfaces of the crystal (e.g. crystal points or wands)*
- *The geometric correspondences of the shapes (e.g. pyramids, spheres, etc.), covered in more detail in the sacred geometry section of this book (page 66)*
- *The visual and physical characteristics of the stones (e.g. seer stones, tumbled vs. raw, etc.)*
- *How the crystal was formed (e.g. under intense pressure or extreme circumstances, such as lava stones)*

As we talked about in the section on choosing your crystals, sometimes the crystal chooses you! When you are selecting a stone, you may be choosing it based not on the specific shape, but instead on the color, correspondences, and type that you are looking for. There are a variety of crystal guides out there that state the properties and energies of different types of crystals, and you may find yourself choosing based on what's available and affordable. Having knowledge of the shapes is helpful, but it doesn't have to limit your choices. Crystals have powerful energies even when they are not a specific shape. The shape simply adds another layer of meaning to your chosen stones.

# A Brief Overview of Crystal Shapes and Uses

| | | |
|---|---|---|
| Clusters | Often used as amplifier stones, to boost and diffuse energies throughout spaces. | |
| Geodes | Popular for internal shifts or transformation. | |
| Points and clusters | Often used for directing energies in a precise way. | |
| Palmstones | Palmstones are exactly as they sound! They are meant to be held and are excellent when used as grounding or meditation tools. | |
| Towers | These work well as energy amplifiers in your spaces. They point upward, which is a visual representation of rising energies. | |

*This is not an exhaustive list, but a good starting point for choosing crystal shapes depending on your intended use.*

| | | |
|---|---|---|
| Spheres | A sphere's surface faces every direction all at once, so spheres are great for evenly distributing energies in a space. They are also often used for scrying, a practice we will cover in more detail in the divination section. | |
| Pyramids | Like towers, these point upward. The pyramid has had great significance through the ages, representing the relationship between humanity and the higher realms. | |
| Hearts | Symbolize love and healing and can also work as objects to hold in mindfulness practices. | |
| Cubes | An exceptionally stable shape, often used for grounding and stabilizing energies. | |
| Ovoid/ Egg shapes | Often used for healing, these shapes correspond with fertility and stability. | |

In general, tumbled and shaped crystals are considered to have a softer energy than raw crystals. Raw crystals are considered to have a more powerful and, well, *raw* energy. You may notice that certain raw crystals look drastically different and less aesthetically dazzling than tumbled ones.

When choosing your crystals, shape can be important for functionality. For example, you probably aren't going to fit a large tower or geode into a charm bag.

If you want an on-the-go option, you may choose a piece of crystal jewelry or a tumbled stone that can fit in your pocket. These practical considerations are important when selecting a shape. Again, though, the shape is not necessarily the be-all and end-all, so don't fret if you cannot find a stone with a specific shape.

# Safety Considerations

Crystals are beautiful, unique, and powerful, but they are not all safe!

Safety issues can arise depending on the type of crystal used—and *how* it is being used. For example:

- *Not all crystals are safe to be handled.*
- *Not all crystals are safe to put in water.*
- *Some crystals may pose a choking hazard for children or pets.*
- *None of your stones should ever be ingested.*
- *Some crystals are sourced in a way that poses ethical hazards to people or the planet.*

## Safety First

Some crystals are toxic and can cause harm. These are typically NOT the ones that are sold in your local metaphysical shop. However, it's important to note that just because something is natural, it does not always mean it is safe. When we buy crystals in a shop and use them in our mindfulness practices, we must make sure we use them safely. They may be safe to handle or display, but it doesn't mean they are harmless in all conditions. For example, some crystals are dangerous if crushed (powdered crystals can be a hazard for inhalation), and others are dangerous when placed in water that you are going to drink or bathe in.

When trying to determine what you can and cannot do with your stones, it is imperative to do your research. Consult crystal guides or encyclopedias, seek out information from a trusted expert and be knowledgeable about the general "dos and don'ts" of working with crystals.

The **Mohs hardness scal**e can be helpful when determining what you can and cannot do with your crystals. This scale classifies different minerals by their hardness. Softer crystals may pose a hazard in certain conditions if they dissolve in water, or if they can be crushed or broken easily. The Mohs scale can also help you make decisions about crystal care and storage, for example, knowing which stones can be stored together without damaging each other.

## Mohs Hardness Scale

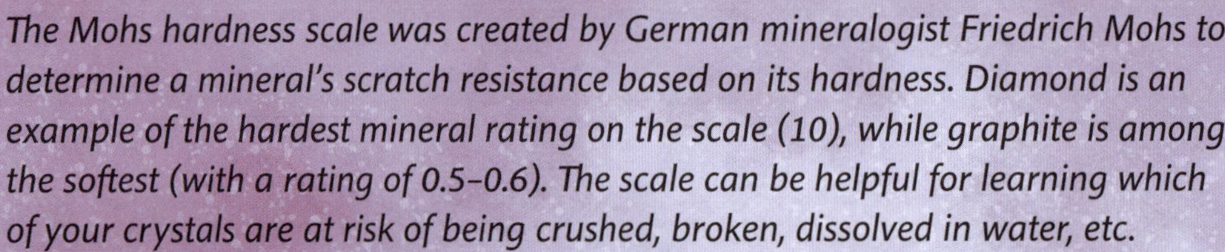

*The Mohs hardness scale was created by German mineralogist Friedrich Mohs to determine a mineral's scratch resistance based on its hardness. Diamond is an example of the hardest mineral rating on the scale (10), while graphite is among the softest (with a rating of 0.5–0.6). The scale can be helpful for learning which of your crystals are at risk of being crushed, broken, dissolved in water, etc.*

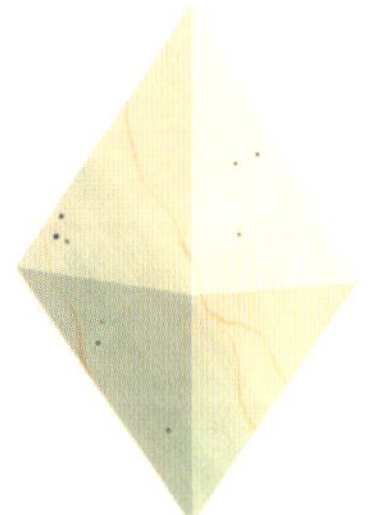

## Crystal Never-Evers

There are certain specific rules that can help you engage with your crystals safely:

- *Never ever ingest or inhale your crystals.*
- *Never ever make gem-infused waters or elixirs using crystal powders, crystals that are deemed not water-safe, or broken or fractured crystals.*
- *Never ever use crystals that are water soluble in the bath.*
- *Never ever heat up your crystals or put them into fire.*
- *Never ever leave your crystals accessible to kids or pets who may ingest or choke on them.*

All of this isn't intended to scare you off using crystals as a part of your self-care. It is meant to empower you to develop a practice that is safe, high-vibe, and fulfilling.

# Crystal Care and Storage

In order to take the best care of your crystals, you have to understand both their energetic and their physical qualities. Ask yourself the following questions:

## Energetic

- *Am I treating my crystals with respect and storing or caring for them so they can be vibrationally and energetically at their best?*

## Physical

- *Is this crystal soft and at risk of chipping when stored with other crystals?*
- *Can this crystal be left in direct sunlight?*
- *Does this crystal need to be kept dry?*
- *Could this crystal pose a hazard to children or pets in its current storage place?*

There are a variety of ways to store your crystals, and what you choose to do will likely be influenced by your collection—how many you have, what form they are in, their hardness, etc.—and the type of storage and space you have available.

Larger pieces, such as geodes or towers, can often be used as decor or for specific purposes when it comes to directing the energy of the home. We will cover this in more detail in the sections on crystals in the home (page 62) and crystals and protection (page 97). When you work with smaller crystals, you may need to put a little more energy, effort, and thought into storing them in a way that will keep them safe and organized.

Some options to consider for storing smaller crystals:

- ***Display shelves:*** *You can get small, compartmentalized shelves meant specifically for crystal storage, or you can simply arrange your crystals on a shelf if you choose. You may need to dust them more often, and you should make sure your crystals are safe from sunlight if they are at risk of discoloration.*

- ***Using an organizer:*** *An organizer (typically a box divided into compartments) can help keep your crystals orderly and easy to sort through when you need them. This method can also prevent them from damaging each other. Make sure you choose a box that has enough space in each compartment for your specimens.*

- ***Small bags or boxes:*** *Some people like to store their crystals in individual bags or boxes. Depending on the space you have available, this may not always be possible.*

- ***Drawers:*** *There are a variety of storage drawer options. Many desktop organizers can double as crystal storage. Again, keep in mind whether your crystals will be at risk of chipping if stored together.*

- ***Placed loosely in a bowl or dish:*** *This is a great "lazy" way to store crystals that doesn't take up too much space, but be aware that harder stones can chip and damage softer ones. Additionally, your crystals may need to be cleared more often (see page 51), as some people believe that certain crystals should not be stored together for energetic reasons.*

Not all crystals have the same physical and energetic properties. For example:

- **Crystal hardness:** *The Mohs hardness scale will give you a clue as to which crystals will likely break down in water or be at higher risk of damage. This is important info to have when it comes to crystal care and storage, as some stones are softer than others, and storing them with other, harder stones could cause breakage.* Some examples of harder crystals are aquamarine and quartz.

- **Crystals and water solubility:** *Not all crystals can be safely placed in water. This includes cleansing your crystals with water, using them in the bath, and using them to make elixirs. Some crystals that are lower on the Mohs hardness scale are likely to dissolve, break down, or become hazardous when submerged.* Some examples of softer crystals that are NOT water-safe are selenite, turquoise, and fluorite. Some examples of crystals that ARE water-safe (but not for extended submerging) are clear quartz, amethyst, and black tourmaline.

- **Crystals and sunlight:** *Some crystals will lose their vibrancy and break down in direct sunlight. They may fade in color, crack, or become brittle. Make sure you research whether your crystals are sun safe before using solar energy to cleanse or recharge your crystals.* Some examples of crystals that will not do well in direct sunlight are citrine, amethyst, and calcite.

**Remember:** caring for your crystals is not just about making sure that your crystals are organized or stored in the right place. Crystals are meant to be worked with in a dynamic and interactive way to ensure their vibrations have the maximum positive impact. You should also cleanse your crystals both physically and energetically, connect with them, and treat them with respect and reverence. When you do, you may find that they are a potent tool for your wellness!

# Cleansing and Charging Your Crystals

Cleansing and charging your crystals on a regular, continual basis allows you to engage with them in a reciprocal way and get the most out of your workings with them. As we've already covered, if you approach these stones in a manner that is devoid of magic and meaning, then you will likely find them to be nothing more than pretty rocks! But when you open to their potential as wellness tools, with their own energies and attributes—and treat them accordingly—you will begin to see all that they have to offer. There is a very good reason why some consider these stones to be living beings!

Cleansing and charging your crystals is the process of clearing and reinvigorating their energy. For example, if you have been working with a particular rose quartz stone to help you move through a challenging time, eventually the stone will need a "refresh" to make sure it continues to be a healing force, rather than just picking up and holding on to the accumulated energy it is meant to transmute. Similarly, if you have a quartz cluster that is being used as a home ward, it should be cleansed on a regular basis to make sure it's not collecting dust or other household debris, and to make sure it is vibrating at the best, most efficient frequency to do its job.

Simple methods for cleansing and charging your crystals include:

- ***Smoke cleansing*** *is when you take sacred cleansing smoke of some sort (typically from incense or herb bundles) and pass it over your crystals to "wash" them. You can waft or blow the smoke over your collection or take your larger crystals and pass them through the smoke. Just be mindful of the considerations we covered earlier in the chapter on safety, and never place your crystals into a fire or expose them to extreme heat.*

- ***Burying:*** *Great news for the dirt worshippers among us: one easy way to cleanse and charge your crystals is by simply burying them in earth. This is a beautiful way to ground their energy. Obviously, if you are burying them* *outside, you will want to be very careful not to bury them so deep that you lose them! A simpler method is to bury the crystals in the soil of your house plants, as you will likely be able to keep track of them pretty easily and it doesn't require access to land. Some would argue that when you use this method, you should bury them for a longer period, but it really depends on what workings you're cleansing and recharging from.*

- ***Water*** *is a great way to cleanse your crystals, both energetically and practically—removing negative energies as well as surface dirt or dust. That said, you will have to ensure that the crystals you are cleansing are water-safe. Make sure to consult the Mohs hardness scale for the crystals you are working with to ensure you don't accidentally dissolve or damage them. Due to its cleansing properties, salt water is sometimes used as a cleansing agent. You will need to make sure this is a safe option for your crystals, as salt water is not the best choice for some stones.*

- ***Moonlight or sunlight:*** *Some shamanic traditions view crystals as the physical manifestation of light itself. By this token, it makes sense to cleanse and charge your crystals with light—either the light of the moon or the light of the sun. Again, make sure that the crystals you are using can safely be in direct light without being damaged. A bonus when using moonlight is that you can ensure you are charging your crystals on a regular basis by aligning with the moon cycle (every 28 days).*

## How often to cleanse and charge your crystals?

*This depends on how often you use your stones and what they have been used for. You should be cleansing them on a routine basis (for example, every moon cycle or monthly), so they do not become stagnant or pick up dense, heavy energies. You will need to forge a relationship with them and learn how to tap into your own inner guidance on this. Ideally, you should be able to connect with your crystals intuitively to tell whether they are in need of a cleanse or energetic refresh.*

PART III

# Prismatic Wellness

*Getting started using crystals as a tool for mindfulness and self-care*

# Crystals and Correspondences

There are so many different types of crystals out there, it can be a challenge to know which one to pick! Luckily, there is a simple way to choose between them depending on your purpose: **to look at their correspondences**.

Correspondences are connections or similarities between things. (You may have heard of the Hermetic principle "as above, so below.") For our purposes, the correspondences of crystals are the qualities, characteristics, and energetic properties that are considered to be vibrationally or energetically equivalent to other things. Given the rich history of crystals in human culture, over time a wide range of correspondences have been noted for each crystal.

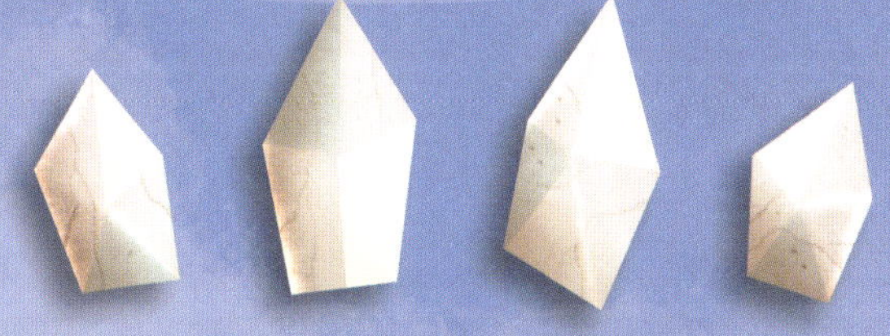

These may include:

*Color correspondences* Different colors of crystals are associated with different energetic properties—for example, pink stones correspond to the heart, romance, and healing. When choosing a crystal for a specific purpose, you can look at color correspondences to help you choose the stone that will work best for what you need.

*Shape correspondences* Each crystal may have properties deriving from its shape on a molecular level, but, as we noted in the section on crystal shapes, the overall shape of the crystal itself also plays a role—for example, pyramid-shaped crystals are associated with our connection to the divine, as they have a stable, grounded base that points upward to the heavens.

## Chakra system correspondences

Certain crystals are considered to correspond to specific energy centers of the body and can be used to rebalance those centers, especially when worn or placed directly on the body—for instance, wearing a lapis lazuli necklace for throat chakra alignment. The Chakra System is originally from Yogic traditions, and refers to different energy centers in the body that may need balancing for optimal spiritual and energetic wellness.

## Body system correspondences and emotional healing

Certain crystals are associated with different body parts or systems and can be used as supplemental tools to help with managing those areas. Similarly, some crystals correspond to mental or emotional states and can be used as part of your self-care strategy to support healing in those areas—for example, crystals for anxiety or grief.

**Astrological correspondences** Like crystals, there are many correspondences involved with astrology. Each sign of the zodiac has its own features, characteristics, archetypal qualities, strengths, and weaknesses, and associated crystals that can be utilized to restore harmony.

**Elemental** Elemental correspondences have been noted throughout human history when working with crystals. The classical elements are earth, air, fire, and water, and each of these has a rich body of their own correspondences. You can choose crystals based on which elements you're trying to realign—for example, celestite corresponds with air.

This is by no means an exhaustive list. There are a variety of other correspondences out there that you may choose to use in your crystal practice, but this list should get you started and on your way.

When using crystal correspondences, it's important to first get a sense of what you are trying to achieve (your intention), or what you are trying to bring back into harmony.

Some examples could be:

- *If you are looking to call in LOVE, you may choose rose quartz. Rose quartz is pink and has the color correspondences of love and romance. It also corresponds to the heart center in the chakra system.*
- *If you are looking to call in ABUNDANCE, you may choose stones that are green, as this color corresponds to wealth and vitality. You may also choose to use stones that are associated with the earth element, which governs the material world, the home, and prosperity.*

One of the hardest things to master when getting into crystals is that there are endless threads of learning and lore associated with their use. Correspondences can be an intoxicating gateway into other modalities and systems that can be used in tandem with crystals. Tapping into these correspondences will help guide your practice.

# Programming Your Crystals

Programming your crystals is essentially the process of infusing the stones with your intention.

For example, if you wanted a crystal to lend you strength during a job interview, you would spend some time connecting with the crystal to activate it for this purpose. If you wanted to program a crystal to be a home ward, you would similarly spend some time "priming" it with your intention.

There are a variety of ways to program a crystal, but the essential thing to know is that you have your own personal energy that can flow into your stone, imbuing it with your unique desire or what you are trying to call in.

## Simple Steps to Program Your Crystals

*First, establish what you want to program your crystal for. What is your intention? What are you trying to achieve?*

*Next, choose a crystal based on the energetic properties and intentions that work best for your intended purpose (see Part IV for guidance about specific crystals and their properties).*

*Cleanse and clear your crystal so that it is freshly energized for programming. You do not want to use a crystal that is energetically stagnant or carrying lingering energies.*

*Ground your own energy (see page 69) and hold your crystal or use your hands to direct energy toward it. State your intention aloud to your crystal. Go further and visualize your desire, and how it would look and feel to have it come to fruition in your life. Let the emotions associated with this wash over you as you direct your energy into the crystal.*

It’s very important to program your crystal so it’s ready for the “job” it is being tasked with. This process also allows you, the practitioner, to get clear on your own focus and hold it at the front and center of your own awareness, so you can also align to the energies you’re seeking!

# Crystals in the Home

Because crystals are visually stunning, they are often used in the home in ways that could at first be mistaken for simple decor. But from small, tumbled stones to large, glittering geodes, crystals are a beautiful and vibey way to enhance the energy of your spaces.

You can keep crystals around the home in a variety of different ways, and you can be as intentional or as casual as you wish. Here are some possibilities you may want to consider if you are new to keeping crystals in the home:

*Altars* Altars are dedicated spaces for arranging sacred items. Altars can hold offerings for deities, or special items that are energizing, activating, or comforting for you, or that are dedicated to specific purposes or intentions. Altars can be as versatile as you need them to be. Creating small altars where you can lay your crystals for specific purposes can be a beautiful way to keep crystals around the home while benefiting from their special energetic properties.

***Wards*** Wards are a form of protection magic that act as a defense of your person, spaces, or home. Crystal items such as suncatchers, towers, or geodes can act as wards if they are programmed for that particular purpose. To make a stone a ward, you must program it as a protector of your home, and this intention can be amplified by using crystals that correspond with this purpose, such as protection or shielding stones.

## To direct energy flow

Every house has its own layout and energy, and we can use crystals to help direct the energy flow around the home in a variety of ways. For example, some people like to arrange protection or cleansing crystals by the doorways to keep the home safe from the energetic baggage of visitors or the outside world. If you want to use crystals to direct the energy flow of your home, it's important to get to know the "personality" of your spaces and how they are used. For instance, if you want your bedroom to be a calm sanctuary for meditation or sleep, you may decide to use calming and grounding crystals in that space.

***Feng shui*** Feng shui is an ancient Chinese practice of directing energy flow. In feng shui, it is believed that all spaces have qi (pronounced chi), a dynamic energy, and that the flow of this energy can be directed by the way that spaces are arranged. Because feng shui works with the elemental forces, crystals that have correspondences to specific elements can be placed in specific positions to ensure the best level of energy flow for the home. Since feng shui is an ancient system with a rich lore, for best results, you may want to read more about it to make the most of utilizing crystals with this modality.

Each home and each space within it has a different personality and unique energy flow. In modern Western culture, we tend to think of our spaces as being "dead" areas, instead of viewing them as energetically alive and dynamic. The character of your home is determined by the people who live there, the events that take place there, and the energies present within. If you want to start using crystals in your home, it can be good to get a sense of the characteristics and vibe of your space.

Although the way you use crystals in your space may be totally unique to you and your needs and intentions, the following are some areas with energetic significance in most homes:

- ***Doorways and entryways:*** *You may want to use protective or shielding stones in entryways, particularly if you often have people coming in and out of the home.*
- ***Kitchen or gathering spaces:*** *Crystals that correspond with love, friendship, or creativity are good options for the social spaces of your home.*
- ***Bedrooms:*** *Protection stones, stones that enhance calm or relaxation, and dream stones are good options for the place where you sleep.*

One thing that's important to note is that stones that are placed in the home can be easy to overlook when it's time to cleanse or refresh your crystals! Make sure you set a schedule (the moon cycle can be useful as a predictable marker) to ensure you get the best results from the crystals in your home.

## Try this

***Make a list of the spaces in your home and what energies or vibes you would like them to have. Find crystals with correspondences that align with these, and program them to help you achieve your aims.***

# Crystals and Sacred Geometry

*Sacred geometry* refers to the foundational patterns and shapes we see over and over again in the natural world. These are often understood through science and mathematics, and can be viewed as fundamental structures that determine the organization of nature, from snowflakes to the gravitational orbits of celestial bodies!

Geometry plays a role in the crystal conversation in a few ways. On one hand, the molecular structures of crystals themselves reflect sacred geometry. Recall the section in Part I on crystal lattice patterns? Some people believe that these patterns have different vibrational frequencies that correspond to specific properties.

The most common way to employ sacred geometry in crystal self-care practices is through the use of **crystal grids**. Crystal grids are intentional arrangements of crystals into geometrical patterns that are meant to amplify and/or direct energies and aid in manifestation. Crystal grids can be complex, but arranging your crystals into basic shapes can also be helpful. Although there are a wide variety of crystal grid templates and products available that you can use to craft your grids into specific sacred geometrical shapes, you should feel free to wing it without having to purchase any special items—even arranging stones into a simple spiral shape will have benefits!

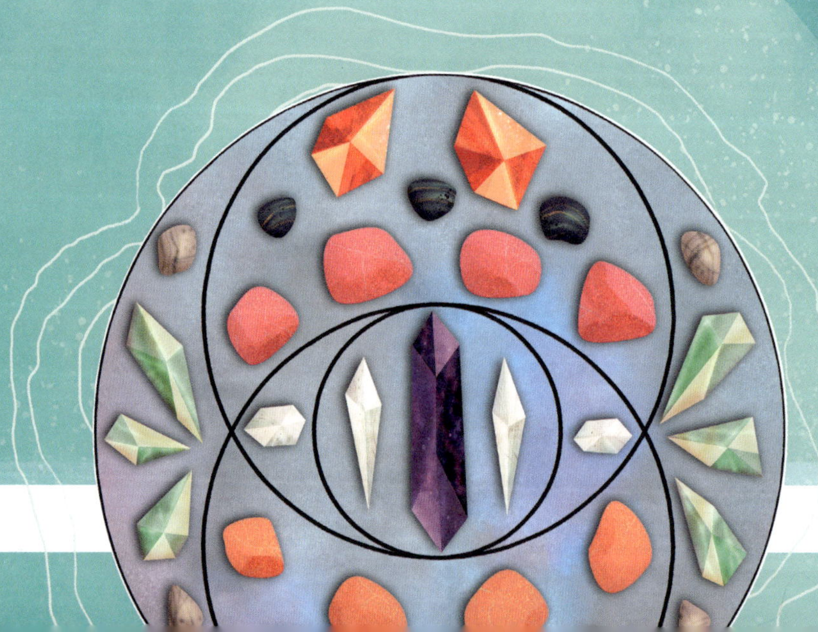

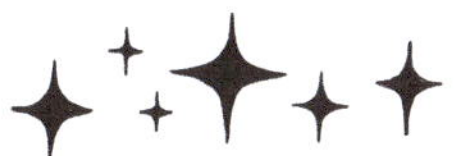

# Using Crystal Grids

A crystal grid is an arrangement of stones that is set up for a specific purpose or intention. There are a variety of ways to set up a grid, but here are some general steps:

- *When crafting a crystal grid, it is important to remember that you should start by getting clarity on your intention—what is it that you are trying to do or achieve with your grid?*
- *Next, you will want to choose which crystals have the kind of properties and correspondences you are looking for. It's important to keep in mind that in a crystal grid, your stones will be working together for a common good. Some crystals may be chosen as amplifiers for others, while others may be chosen for their own specific properties. The energy of your grid will shift depending on which crystals are placed where and in what shape.*
- *Most crystal grids have a main center stone, which anchors and pulls together the energies of the surrounding crystals on the grid. You can program this crystal with your specific intention for best results.*
- *Next, take your other stones and arrange them in a symmetrical pattern around your center stone. You can use specific, more complex shapes (such as the Flower of Life pattern) or arrange them intuitively. It may take some re-working until you are happy with the pattern and energy flow of your grid.*
- *Finally, you will want to activate your grid. This can be done through energy work, using your hands or fingers to "connect" the energies of the crystals on your grid.*

Crystal grids are typically set up to be used for longer periods of time—days or even weeks. As such, you will want to periodically reactivate them for best results.

# Common Sacred Geometrical Crystal Grid Patterns and Their Correspondences

| Pattern | Correspondence |
| --- | --- |
| Flower of Life | New beginnings and the interconnection of everything in nature. |
| Hexagram | Equilibrium and balance. |
| Circle | Unity and wholeness. |
| Square | Grounding energy, stability. |
| Fibonacci Spiral | A specific spiral shape that utilizes the golden ratio. This pattern corresponds with beauty and harmony. |
| Metatron's Cube | A combination of interlinked shapes that is said to include all the base geometrical shapes in its design. This pattern corresponds with protection and harmony and is sometimes referred to as the "blueprint of creation." |

# Crystals and Energetic Grounding

Since many stones are used for grounding, pairing crystals with meditation can be a great way to enhance your meditation practice.

All living things, including Earth itself, have an electromagnetic field. As we discussed at the beginning of this book, crystals have been used throughout the ages as tools for realigning and directing these energy fields.

Earthing is the practice of "grounding your energy" by allowing your field to interface with that of Earth. Typically, earthing is approached by allowing your bare feet or body to come into direct contact with the ground. Doing so is said to stabilize your energy, inviting calm, strength, and peace into your body and mind. Grounding with crystals essentially uses the same principle but in an "as above, so below" kind of way. Crystals are formed and mined from the earth and can be used to bring grounding and earth element energy into your practices!

As we covered earlier, some crystals have the capability to conduct electricity. The popularity of crystals has endured for so long due to the belief and anecdotal evidence that crystals can shift humans' vibrational frequencies in a beneficial way. When it comes to using crystals for energetic grounding, it is important to use ones whose correspondences are for serene, stabilizing energies. These can be used as part of your meditation or grounding practices to help calm, soothe, and recalibrate a fried-out or overactive nervous system.

Even when it comes to choosing a crystal in the shop, some people assert that they can "feel" the charge of a stone while holding it, or that they can feel it recalibrating their energy. To use these in a grounding or meditative process will add an extra boost to your efforts to stay calm, cool, and collected!

There are a variety of ways in which you can use crystals for grounding or meditation—you are only limited by your imagination! Here are some general steps to help you begin:

- *Choose crystals that correspond to calm, healing, or stabilizing energies.*
- *Sit in a quiet space where you are unlikely to be disturbed. Sitting cross-legged, if you're able to, is better than lying down, to avoid falling asleep.*
- *Hold your crystals in your palm (or one in each hand) and begin breathing deeply. Allow your thoughts to come and go without getting too hung up on them.*
- *If it's helpful, visualize the energies of the crystals and your breath as a watery light that washes over your body and the surrounding electrical field.*
- *As you breathe in, absorb this cleansing and healing light.*
- *As you exhale, imagine any anxious or restless energies being diffused out of your body.*

This is one way to meditate with crystals—but remember that it is not the ONLY way!

You may also use a crystal grid for grounding and meditation, or place crystals directly on your body as you relax and move into a state of mindfulness. You can use stones in meditative or reflective bath rituals, and carry them on your person to help you remain calm and stable when in new, unfamiliar, or triggering spaces. There are many ways to incorporate crystals into your meditative practices, just make sure whichever way you choose works for you.

# Crystals and Setting Up Sacred Space

Although crystals can be used for many purposes in your sacred self-care rituals, one of the simplest ways to incorporate them into your routines consistently is to use them for establishing your sacred space.

Setting up a sacred space is energetically helpful and can also help you become psychologically primed to engage in your spiritual or self-care work. When you take the time to set up your space, you are creating an energetic boundary that exists outside the realm of mundane or everyday reality. Ideally, when you set up sacred space to engage in meditation, divination, rituals, or whatever other workings you are about to engage in, you should do so with the understanding that you are not going to be on the same plane of consciousness that you are in when cleaning the bathroom or doing something similarly ordinary.

To set up sacred space is to engage in a physical act that backs up your intention!

## Simple Ways to Establish Sacred Space Using Crystals

- *Choose stones that correspond with your intention or that will help you establish your space. Protection stones such as smoky quartz, black tourmaline, or amethyst are good for this.*
- *Make sure that your stones are cleared and programmed for this use. Your crystals can be scattered around the room, used to create a circle, or set up on a crystal grid or altar. As you set them into place, speak your intention to them.*
- *If you have larger crystals in your home used for decor, as wards or to help the energy flow, you may want to refresh them by clearing and programming them anew. The idea is that the space will be set up in such a way that it is different from any other time when you are not engaging in magical work.*
- *Once your sacred space is established, take the time to ground your own energy and get a sense for the vibe of the space. Check in with your intuition to see if it feels right, or if you need to do further work to prepare the space.*
- *Visualization is a wonderful tool for aligning your own energy, as well as for working with crystals in tandem with your purpose. Sit comfortably and take some deep, cleansing breaths, then imagine that the crystals you set up are expanding energetically to fill the room with protective light. You can visualize breathing the energy of these stones in and out.*
- *Once you are done with your workings, make sure to close your space. Set the intention to take down your sacred space, and back this up either by stating your intention aloud or by collecting your things to put them away.*
- *Make sure to clear and cleanse your stones afterward so they will be ready to help you next time you need them.*

# Wearing Crystals

Wearing your crystals is an excellent and aesthetically pleasing way to keep the energies of your stones close no matter where you go. There are a variety of ways to wear your crystals, but the commonest way is as jewelry.

Wearable crystal options range from beaded bracelets to bellybutton rings—and everything in between! Wearing crystals close to or touching the body is a potent way to align with their energies. As discussed in the section on correspondences, different crystals have different energetic properties, and they can shift our frequency in a number of ways. When choosing crystal jewelry you may want to consider the following:

- *Opt for jewelry that is comfortable and safe for you to wear. If you are not usually comfortable wearing jewelry, you may want to find another way to keep your crystals close.*
- *Choose crystals that correspond with what you are trying to achieve—for example, wearing a rose quartz necklace that falls close to your anatomical heart to help open or align your heart chakra.*
- *Consider the part of your body where your jewelry will sit—for example, wearing an abundance crystal on your dominant hand may correspond with taking action that could bring about success.*
- *Pay attention when combining crystal jewelry. You can "stack" your wearable crystals and benefit from the different energies of all of them, but make sure you are intentional with which stones you choose to wear together, so that the aims of each complement and don't neutralize one another.*

# Wards, Amulets, and Talismans

*Wards* We have talked a little bit about wards in the home, but an item of crystal jewelry can also act as a ward. This would be a piece of protective jewelry worn to stave off negative energies, bad luck, or any other icky vibes. For example, a person may wear a specific necklace when going to large, crowded spaces to protect themselves energetically.

*Amulets* An amulet is an object that is meant to protect and lend power or good luck to the wearer. You can intentionally program a piece of jewelry to act as an amulet, particularly if you use a stone that corresponds to the kind of power or good fortune you are trying to call in. For example, you could wear a strength or confidence amulet when doing a job interview.

*Talismans* Talismans are similar to wards and amulets. They are essentially pieces of jewelry that are designed to bring good fortune, healing, or power to the wearer while also repelling bad energy. A talisman can be as simple as a good luck bracelet or keyring.

Check out the section on programming your crystals for more information on how to go about preparing a piece of jewelry to act as a ward, amulet, or talisman. One important thing to note is that since it will be worn on your person and will encounter the many different energies and environments that you do, it would be wise to conduct your energetic clearings on a frequent basis to ensure that the crystals stay effective and don't accumulate stagnant energies.

Although crystal jewelry is the most obvious way to wear your stones, there are a variety of other ways that you can carry your crystals with you. Putting a crystal in a pocket or in your bra can allow you to hold its energy close, yet without the stone being visible to others. There are also a variety of new products on the market that incorporate wearable crystals. For example, there are certain brands of clothing that have crystals sewn in, so that they are kept close to specific energy centers of the body. Alternatively, you may opt to carry crystals in charm bags, shamanic pouches, or even a purse—anything goes!

# Bathing with Crystals

Crystals can be a wonderful way to enhance your bath rituals, but it's vital to use them properly for best results and to stay safe!

Before we dig in on crystals themselves, let's talk about bath rituals. Bath rituals are self-care practices where the bathtub is used as a transformational container for whatever it is you are trying to achieve. Spiritual baths have been a sacred practice for humans since ancient times, and the trend continues to this day. Whether for spiritual cleansing, protection, or emotional healing, bath rituals allow you to use the energetic correspondences of things like herbs, oils, and yes, crystals, to energetically and vibrationally infuse the water with your intent.

In Part II, we talked about the importance of determining whether your stones are water soluble and how the Mohs hardness scale may help with this. There are crystals that you can safely place in water, but there are also many that are not safe to bathe with. Many crystal guides will list whether or not crystals are water-safe. However, if you want to do a bath ritual using crystals without submerging your stones, there are a few super simple ways to do this!

*Placing crystals around your bath* Crystals can be used as part of your ritual bath space without having to actually submerge them in water. For example, you can place your crystals around the bathroom or the outside of the bathtub, on a bath tray or even inside the empty tub as a way to prime your space.

*Using crystals to charge other items in your ritual*
Crystals can be used to charge your bath salts, oils, candles, etc. with whatever energetic properties you are hoping to bring to your ritual. Typically, this involves placing a crystal on your items for a set period (for example, overnight) and using

visualization or energy work to infuse the items with the vibration of that particular crystal's correspondences. We'll cover this in the section on charging other items with crystals (page 88).

## Bath-Safe Crystal Suggestions

*The following are some common and easily sourced crystals that are water-safe in most conditions. Please note that tumbled stones are best, so that you do not scratch the surface of your bathtub:*

***Quartz*** *An excellent amplifier stone that works for many rituals, including cleansing and purifying baths.*

***Rose quartz*** *A stone that corresponds with love and the heart center. Good for love, self-love, or glamor rituals.*

***Amethyst*** *A calming stone that corresponds with intuition and spirituality. Great for meditative healing and spiritual baths.*

*Although these are bath-safe based on the Mohs hardness scale, there's a small chance they may crack in hot water. Make sure to watch your crystals carefully for signs of breakage to keep yourself safe!*

# Crystals and Divination

Divination is the practice of attempting to "see" into the future. Humanity has a rich history of divination across cultures, and crystals are just one tool that we can use for this purpose!

Divination practices are those that people use to gain some sort of otherwise hidden information that can help us foresee what is to come or glean extra knowledge about confusing or unknown circumstances. There are countless methods of divining, but we are going to cover a few that pair well with or utilize crystals.

First off, when looking at crystal correspondences for divination, you may want to choose stones that pair well with intuition, psychic ability, or the third-eye chakra. These crystals can be used to establish your sacred space, or to shift your energy to a place that is intuitively tapped-in and energetically open.

Although crystals can be used in tandem with other methods, there are many ways that you can use crystals themselves as your divination tool. Here are a few examples.

## Some Specialized Crystal Tools of Divination

### Crystal balls and seer stones

*Seer stones are crystals that typically have some sort of a window-like surface that you are meant to gaze into for the purpose of gaining visions or mental imagery or knowledge of some sort. Crystal balls are crystals that are polished and shaped into spheres for the same purpose.*

**Pendulums** *Pendulums are typically crystal points suspended on a chain and used as a method of divining by posing questions and seeing which direction and in what manner the pendulum spins. When working with a pendulum, you must first spend some time programming it and building a relationship to establish a language, i.e. which direction of spin means yes and which means no.*

**Scrying mirrors** *Scrying mirrors are mirrors that can be gazed into for divining purposes. There are a few types of scrying mirrors—technically you can even use water!—but the smooth, reflective surface of obsidian is commonly used for this purpose.*

**Crystal runes or charm sets** *Runes are stones carrying ancient symbols that represent different qualities or energies. Charm sets are sets of objects with specified meanings attached. They are shaken and scattered, and you can then draw conclusions based on which pieces land where. Although not all runes and charm sets are made from crystals, there are crystal-based sets available, or you can create your own. The key is to determine which stones represent which aspects (whether that be areas of your life, particular energies, etc.), and to set yourself parameters for how you will read them. Using a surface that is separated into different areas is fairly common, as you can then interpret each stone's position in tandem with where it falls.*

**When divining** *If you want to get started with any divination practice, it's important to do the following:*

- *Set up your space and establish your intention.*
- *Ensure that your own energy is cleared and grounded. You can do this with crystals or grounding practices such as breathwork or meditation.*
- *Get into an altered state of mindful relaxation.*
- *As you engage in your divination, pay attention to any insights from your intuition, such as body sensations, mental images, sounds, thoughts, and other feelings that may arise. The more you engage in connecting with your intuition, the more you will understand the bodily sensations and messages that are speaking to you!*

# Crystals and Sound Healing

Sound healing is another energetic healing modality that is gaining more and more popularity. It is based on the idea that sound vibrations can have a beneficial effect on our physical, energetic, and emotional bodies.

As a type of frequency medicine, sound healing typically uses specific instruments to achieve different desired results. It is not just about how the instruments are played in the moment; how they are made and what they are made of also play an important role.

Crystal and sound healing are closely linked, as they are both types of frequency healing that lean into the idea of an energetic body that can be manipulated for positive results. In fact, there are many sound healing instruments that directly use crystals. For example:

- *Crystal singing bowls are a popular sound healing and meditation tool. These bowls are typically created using quartz, but there are other types of crystal-infused bowls that incorporate different crystals, such as carnelian, lapis lazuli, and more.*

- *Crystal pyramids can be chimed around a person's body as part of a sound healing exercise.*

- *Chimes can incorporate crystals as part of their design to amplify the sound frequency energies.*

If you are interested in pairing crystals with sound healing, there is no need to go out and spend a bundle on a crystal bowl set or other specialized tools. As with many other modalities, you can use crystals to set up the sacred space you are going to be using. You can choose specific crystals based on their energetic properties or correspondences, and place them around your sound healing space or directly onto your body.

# Crystals and Astrology

As we discussed earlier, one of the modalities that can be used in tandem with crystals is astrology.

The topic of astrology is so vast and compelling that it has endured as a source of fascination since ancient times. For our purposes, though, we'll keep it brief. Astrology is the study of the cosmos' interaction with and influence on us here on Earth. In astrology, the time of a person's birth is used to formulate a birth chart—a snapshot of the locations of the planets and celestial bodies at the exact moment they were born. This information tells us our zodiac sign. This is the constellation that the sun was in when we were born.

Each zodiac sign has its own archetypal qualities and characteristics, associated lore, strengths, weaknesses, and more. It also corresponds to specific elements, body systems, and ruling planets, and has its own positive and detrimental qualities. There is a rich body of information in astrology that corresponds to each of the zodiac signs, planets, and houses, and which determines how they interact or express themselves based on where they are found in your unique birth chart.

Certain crystals correspond with each of the zodiac signs based on the qualities and characteristics of that particular sign. Some crystals might be used to amplify those qualities, whereas others might be used to ground the energies or make up for qualities that may be lacking. For instance, Capricorn is seen as a sign that is driven and ambitious, so black tourmaline may be a good stone to ground those energies and to ward off any pessimistic negative thinking that can come with the very disciplined archetype of this sign.

## The Zodiac Signs and Their Common Characteristics

The following is a very brief, general overview of each of the signs and their corresponding elements, along with their common light and shadow characteristics:

### Aries (fire)

Aries are typically described as energetic, courageous leaders on the light side. On the shadow side, they can be prone to anger or display a competitive nature.

### Taurus (earth)

Taurus energy is very earthy, sensual, and loyal. On the shadow side, Taurus are often described as prone to stubbornness or lacking forward motion.

### Gemini (air)

Gemini is a sign that is often described as curious, intelligent, and socially apt. On the shadow side, Gemini energy can be unpredictable and impulsive.

### Cancer (water)

Cancer energy is commonly described as emotional and nurturing. On the shadow side, Cancer is often associated with moodiness and holding grudges.

### Leo (fire)

Leo energy is dynamic, confident, and fun. On the shadow side, Leo can be prone to arrogance or selfish pride.

### Virgo (earth)

Virgo energy is practical and associated with loyalty and striving to do what's right. The shadow side of this is that Virgo can be nit-picky and overly judgmental.

### Libra (air)
Libras are communicative, harmonious, and charming. On the shadow side, Libras may be manipulative or unrealistic, as their desire for harmony can make them resistant to being honest with themselves and others.

### Scorpio (water)
Scorpio energy is intense, passionate, and full of emotional depth. On the shadow side, Scorpio energy can be vengeful, manipulative, and possessive.

### Sagittarius (fire)
Sagittarius energy is feisty, playful, and adventurous. On the shadow side, Sagittarius can be harshly direct and a bit reckless.

### Capricorn (earth)
Capricorn energy is driven, disciplined, and ambitious. On the shadow side, Capricorns are prone to being overly negative in their thinking and can be stubbornly rigid in their mindset.

### Aquarius (air)
Aquarius energy is unique, original, and innovative. The shadow side of Aquarius energy is that they can be cold and detached.

### Pisces (water)
Pisces energy is sensitive and empathetic. On the shadow side, Pisces are often described as being overly idealistic, delusional, and indecisive.

When looking at each sign's light and shadow traits, you can begin to form an idea of the kinds of crystals you might want to use either to enhance the positive light aspects, or to ground or counter the detrimental shadow aspects.

### Ask yourself
***Which zodiac sign are you? Which qualities would you like to amplify and which would you like to counter?***

# Crystals and Tarot

Due to their popularity in witchy, spiritual and New Age circles, crystals and Tarot mesh together well, and they are often used to complement one another!

For those who may be new to Tarot, here's a quick rundown. Tarot is a divination system composed of cards charged with symbols and archetypes. A standard Tarot deck is typically composed of 78 cards, each featuring imagery and carrying a particular meaning and a symbolic set of correspondences. The set is divided into two parts: the Major Arcana and the Minor Arcana. The Minor Arcana is separated into four categories (much like the suits of a regular deck of playing cards): Pentacles, Wands, Swords, and Cups. Each of these suits has court cards, again, much like playing cards, with a King, Queen, Page, and Knight. The Major Arcana is made up of 22 powerful archetype cards, from the Fool to the World, which tell a transformational story.

Both crystals and Tarot can be harnessed as tools for your spiritual wellness practices. You can use them separately or in tandem with one another, and like most things in the realm of the spirit, how you choose to go about doing so may be completely intuitive and is totally up to you! That being said, let's look at a few ways you can start doing this, to give you a jumping-off point and a little inspiration that you can customize and play with later.

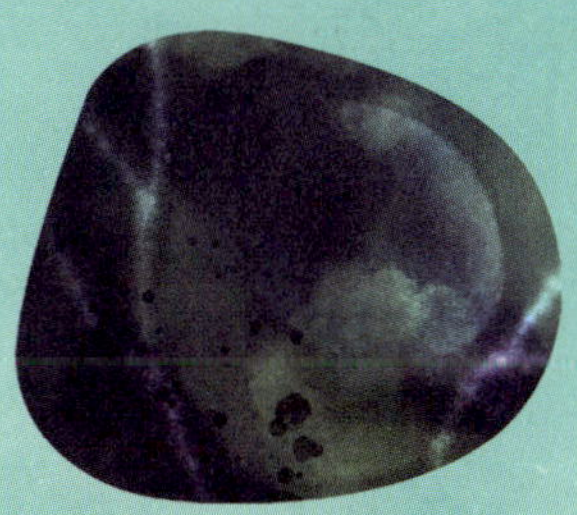

# Using Crystals to Enhance Your Tarot Practices

Some ways you can use your stones to enhance or amplify your Tarot practices include:

- *Using crystals to help establish the energy of your sacred space for connecting with the Tarot.*
- *Using crystals that enhance psychic energies or intuition to help with your readings.*
- *Using crystals to help you anchor in your intentions for your readings and the sorts of answers you are seeking.*
- *Using protective stones such as smoky quartz to keep you energetically safe while you engage in this divination practice.*
- *Using specific stones that correspond with the energies you are reading for—for example, using rose quartz during a love reading.*
- *Assigning a different crystal for each card in a multi-card pick, with each crystal's energy corresponding to the area of life your cards will be reading.*
- *Using your crystals to charge and cleanse your deck.*
- *Choosing particular archetypes to call in—for example, using a specific Tarot card to meditate on and pairing it with a crystal or crystals that correspond to that same vibe.*

In *Cunningham's Encyclopedia of Crystal, Gem & Metal Magic*, author Scott Cunningham outlines a process of creating a "Stone Tarot." This essentially takes the symbolic correspondences and archetypes of the Major Arcana of the Tarot deck and assigns a specific crystal for each to create a "set." With the process he outlines, a person could use their stones in place of, or in tandem with, the traditional Tarot. This is just one example of a practice that utilizes elements of both.

So if you want to use crystals with Tarot, begin by thinking of ways to incorporate both tools in a way that makes sense for you. Just remember your best practices when it comes to energetically clearing and cleansing both your stones and your decks, so that you are working with a clean slate each time. You may want to document your readings and the crystals you used (and how you used them) to get best results and continue nurturing that ongoing relationship with your stones!

# Crystals to Charge Other Items

We've discussed a few different ways to cleanse and charge your crystals, but did you know that because some stones are considered to have amplifying properties, they can be used to charge or activate other crystals? The two most common examples of this are selenite and clear quartz. Selenite is often sold in specific shapes to encourage this use, for example, selenite plates, bowls, and grid plates, typically engraved or etched with sacred geometric designs such as those covered in the section on crystal grids (page 66). In these cases, other crystals can be placed on the selenite surface to clear and charge their energies. Consider it a little boost!

Clear quartz is generally considered to be a good master stone in terms of its cleansing and amplifying properties, which makes it a similarly good option for giving some "oomph" to your other stones. This can be accomplished by placing your crystals within a grid or circle of clear quartz, with the intention of realigning and amplifying the stones' properties for your intended use.

As we saw in the chapter on crystal grids, arranging your crystals in certain patterns can also help to amplify and clear energies for other stones. The best idea if you want to use these methods is to play around and take note of your results, to help you find what works most powerfully for you.

This can also highlight the importance of regularly working with our crystals. Ultimately, we want them to function with the most efficiency and potency that we can muster, particularly when they are interacting not only with us, but with *each other.*

## Cleansing Crystals With Other Crystals

- *If using a selenite plate or bowl, carefully add your other crystals and leave them to charge overnight. You may also do this in tandem with other cleansing methods* *(see page 51).*
- *If using other stones, such as clear quartz, you can try creating a circle of your quartz crystals and placing other stones in the middle.*
- *In the chapter on sound healing, we talked about quartz crystal sound bowls and their cleansing properties. If you have access to crystal bowls, you can leave your crystals nearby as you play for them.*

PART IV

# Crystalline Counsel

## *Stones and practices to troubleshoot hard times*

# Crystals and Anxiety

## Correspondences for Addressing Anxiety

- *The color LIGHT BLUE*
- *The root chakra*
- *The herb chamomile*

## Suggested practices: *Breathwork, meditation, medicinal movement, bath rituals, creating*

Anxiety is a terribly unpleasant condition that can express itself in many ways. In general, it is characterized by heightened body system activation, including fear, restlessness, dread, a racing heart rate, irritability, physical pain (headaches, etc.), and an overall struggle to regulate yourself when activated.

There are many kinds of anxiety, including social anxiety and panic disorders, but what they all seem to have in common is the felt experience of a full-body emergency, activating base functions such as the fight-or-flight response. This has such a profound effect on the body that very few resources are left to help you think clearly. This is why trying to talk yourself down or use logic to move through the experience is often unsuccessful. As anyone who has experienced a panic attack can testify, it is a terrifying experience that can leave a person without the mental and physical reserves needed to calm themselves down.

You can approach tackling anxiety with crystals in a variety of ways depending on your unique circumstances, symptoms, and struggles. For instance, social anxiety that stems from a lack of confidence may be tackled not only with anxiety stones, but also with confidence stones, in order to get to the root of the problem. Similarly, social anxiety is often characterized by a restriction on the voice or throat chakra, which means that in some cases, stones that correspond with this energy center can provide relief. For something like health anxiety, you may look to crystals that work with specific body centers or related physical issues.

The key to troubleshooting anxiety (or any other issue for that matter) starts with having a clear understanding of what you're currently dealing with and how it manifests both physically and mentally, as well as an idea of what it would look like if that was cleared from your life.

## A Suggested Practice

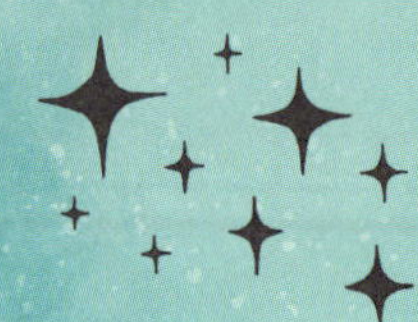

Bath rituals can be a highly potent method of managing anxiety, as the warmth of the water can be very soothing and grounding, allowing the body to relax a little and ease up from the panic and "racing" energy of anxiety.

For this ritual, you will want to fill a bathtub with warm water, adding any extras (bath salts, herbs, etc.) that you like. I would also suggest playing music that is calming and grounding for you, maybe lighting some candles, and to try this when you are unlikely to be disturbed.

Take a crystal that corresponds to anxiety management and program it to help you move through the symptoms the anxiety is bringing up for you. For this bath ritual, I would suggest amethyst, as it is water-safe. Take your crystal and place it in the water and then stir the water with your hand counterclockwise, asking aloud for your anxiety symptoms to be released.

Get into the water and allow yourself to rest and relax. When you are struggling with anxiety, trying to do much more than this can be overwhelming. Just be calm, and let your physical and mental symptoms subside. Focus on your breathing and allow yourself to ease.

# Suggested Crystals for Managing Anxiety

| | | |
|---|---|---|
| *Blue calcite* | A soothing and relaxing stone that can help with anxiety by drawing out negative energy. | |
| *Amber* | A stress reliever and grounding stone that can transmute negative emotion in the body and mind. | |
| *Amethyst* | A serene and spiritual stone that can balance the energies in the body, mind, and spirit. | |
| *Blue lace agate* | A calming and soothing stone that can enhance agate self-expression and communication. | |
| *Rose quartz* | A fundamental crystal for working with matters of the heart; a peaceful and healing stone. | |
| *Howlite* | Calms the mind, helps soothe difficult emotions. | |

# Crystals and Protection

## Correspondences for Protection

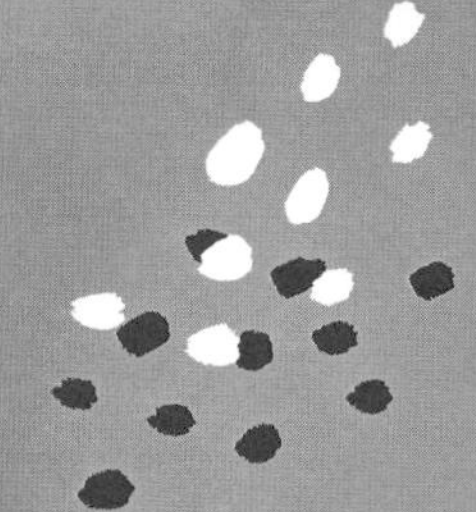

- *The color BLACK*
- *The root chakra*
- *The herb rosemary*

## Suggested practices: *Creating wards and talismans, cleansing and clearing your spaces, journaling and affirmations, boundaries meditations*

One of the most popular ways that crystals are used is for protection. Whether carried on someone's person (such as jewelry or talismans) or set up around the home, crystals are a common tool for directing and clearing energies of both people and their spaces. They have a rich history of use as protective agents in this realm and in the mystical realms (including the astral and the underworld).

In our modern world, it can feel as though an influx of energies and information is barraging us on all sides. It isn't uncommon for people to feel energetically drained and depleted as a result. And that's on top of the individual drains we all experience—things like drama, gossip, and the like. This is why boundaries are so important and stressed in the context of therapy, and why protection work is one of the foundations of spiritual/magical practices and energy work in general.

How a person will work with stones for protection depends on what they are experiencing and dealing with. For some, setting up protections of environment and place (such as wards or regular energetic cleanses) may be a priority, while for others, protections from outside energies such as other people or entities might be more important. Crystals can be used for all manner of protection works, and you will likely need to experiment a little with the specifics of your unique circumstances in order to find what works best for you.

## A Suggested Practice

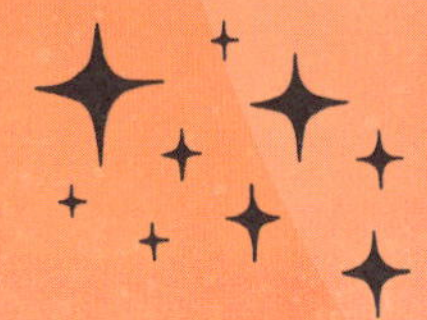

Create a protective charm bag to bring with you when you are out and about. Charm bags are small sachets of items that you can carry with you or throw in your bag to help with certain things you are trying to manifest—in this case, for protection. Charm bags typically include herbs or small items, including crystals or crystal chips, to act as an energetic tether for what you are trying to achieve.

Choose a crystal from the suggested list opposite (smoky quartz is a good one) and add it to your charm bag with other protective items, such as rosemary, lavender, or small trinkets that symbolize protection to you. (Just be mindful of the breakability of the crystal you are using, or you may run the risk of your stone cracking or chipping.) Cleanse and program your stone to act as a protective barrier between you and any unwanted or bad vibes and energies. This can be especially powerful if you are going to be in large crowds of unknown people or in circumstances that may feel decidedly unfriendly.

Carry your charm bag with you to keep you energetically safe and protected as you move through the world. Cleanse and refresh your items and bag often.

# Suggested Crystals for Protection

| | | |
|---|---|---|
| *Smoky quartz* | A cleansing stone that detoxes and transmutes negative energies. | |
| *Black tourmaline* | A protective stone that draws out negative energy and promotes grounding. | |
| *Kunzite* | Energetic protection; a shielding stone that helps relieve stress. | |
| *Black obsidian* | Wards off negative energy and helps realign energies to be more supportive. | |
| *Tiger's eye* | A protective stone with a rich history of use. Helps heal conflicts. | |

# Crystals and Depression

## Correspondences for Working With Depression

- *The color YELLOW*
- *The lower chakras—root, sacral, solar plexus, and heart*
- *The herb lavender*

**Suggested practices:** *Affirmations, bath rituals, journaling, creation, connecting with others*

Depression is a mood disorder that many of us have had intimate experience with—either personally or when supporting others who have struggled. Depression is an insidious condition that can dull the sparkle of life, as its symptoms include lack of interest or joy, persistent feelings of sadness and melancholy, and a variety of physical and mental discomforts. Far from just "being sad," depression is a condition that can feel as if it is sucking the very life out of you. However, there are both medical and practical treatments available that can help provide some relief!

In an energetic sense, depression can feel like the original definition of the word for which the disorder was named: "to be forced into a lower or downward position." The felt experience of it can be crushing. Whether it be a transient depressive episode or persistent dysthymia (a more lingering version of the condition) there is a sensation of "flatness." Mood is flat, perception is flat and, in many cases, expression, hopes, dreams, etc. all feel . . . flat.

As with any other mental disorder, the first order of business should always be to seek help from a doctor, therapist, or other qualified mental health professional. Depression is truly no joke! However, there are always supplemental avenues available for us to support our own healing. Crystals can fit well into this equation.

When it comes to using crystals for depression, it is best to look at what you are currently experiencing. Can you identify the origin of your depression? What are your current symptoms, and how would you like to feel? For example, some depression arises gradually from a general lack of self-esteem, in which case, crystals and inner work related to confidence or self-love would be helpful. For other cases where you may be experiencing a depressive episode due to grief or something similar, you may want to choose crystals or inner work that help resolve the tricky feelings that have arisen as a result of the loss. (There are entries in the following pages on the themes of both self-esteem and grief.)

## A Suggested Practice

Take a tiger's eye crystal (or another of the suggested crystals for depression listed opposite) and spend a few moments each morning holding it and focusing on your breathing. Ask for the strength and vitality of the crystal to activate your body and mind to feel strong, motivated, and positive. Tiger's eye is also a protective stone. As you hold the stone, ask it for its protection, strength, and loving energy. Ask to have eyes to see the joy around you. Ask to have ears to hear the good, and for your voice to speak the good that's all around and within you. Ask for the strength to transmute your woes into growth and healing. Ask for the motivational power to move beyond old conceptualizations of yourself and to embody the brilliant person you are in this moment. Thank the crystal for its protection and for being your ally in this task.

This practice works well in conjunction with gratitude journaling or setting active intentions for positive things to manifest in your life.

## Suggested Crystals for Depression

| | | |
|---|---|---|
| *Tiger's Eye* | Helps to integrate challenging emotions and decrease malaise. | |
| *Moonstone* | Calms emotions, promotes emotional harmony. | |
| *Clear quartz* | A master healer that raises personal vibration. | |
| *Rose quartz* | A soothing stone for the heart energy centers, rose quartz is good for matters of love, including self-love. | |
| *Flower agate* | A supportive stone that helps in moving beyond past harms and old, outdated stories. | |

# Crystals for Experiencing Loss

## Correspondences for Working With Grief and Loss

- *The color GREEN*
- *The root and heart chakras*
- *The flower rose*

**Suggested practices:** *Journaling, connecting with others, bath rituals, meditation, creating*

Life is such a beautiful, transient process, but part of the unique experience of being human is the agonizing experience of loss. Loss can come to us in many forms. We can experience breakups and grief over relationships that fizzle out or fail in a dramatic blaze. We can experience loss and grief when our loved ones pass away. We can experience loss when our dreams or goals appear to be outside of our reach, or if things go spectacularly left of what we had planned. We can feel loss about who we think we are—or transitioning away from who we thought we were. To be alive is to dance with loss, over and over again, in new and different ways.

Loss is truly a painful but necessary part of life itself!

If you are experiencing a loss, there are crystal energies that can support you as you move through the experience. The kinds of crystals you may choose to use—and how you choose to use them—can vary depending on the circumstances. Are you in a state of grief regarding a loved one who has crossed over? Are you experiencing the loss of an outcome you truly wanted? Is there discord in a personal relationship that's tinged with regret or grief? These are questions to ask yourself when troubleshooting loss of all kinds. This will allow you to design a self-care practice to help soothe the experience, as well as enable you to find any other correspondences or elements you can incorporate for targeted healing (for example, a breakup could use correspondences for love and the heart).

## A Suggested Practice

Take an Apache tear crystal (or other crystal suggested for work with grief and loss) and set up a bath ritual to reflect on and soothe your experience of pain. To do this, fill your bathtub with hot water and any additions you would like to include, such as salts, herbs, or flowers (rose works well for this). If you have a bath tray, set it up with your crystal and a candle (do not submerge your stone). Feel free to play any soothing music that will help you stay calm during this process.

Get into the bath and gaze into your candle and hold your crystal. Reflect on the experience you are going through, truly allowing yourself to feel it, making note of the thoughts and emotions that arise, and the beliefs associated with them. Reflect on the transient nature of life, and the archetypal energy of the Wheel of Fortune, the cycles of life that careen us both upward and downward. Visualize the crystal vibrations lending you healing energy, and when you drain the bath, imagine that the physical and mental sensations of the rawness of your grief are merged with the water in the tub as it leaves the vessel and circles into the drain.

Sleep beside your crystal while you move through the stages of your grief, cleansing and clearing it often.

# Suggested Crystals for Loss and Grief

| | | |
|---|---|---|
| *Apache tear* | A comforting stone that helps with processing grief and letting go of painful things. | |
| *Amethyst* | A calming and healing stone that helps dissipate and transmute painful negative emotions. | |
| *Fire opal* | Helps facilitate change and transition and supports letting go of or releasing grief and pain. | |
| *Rhodonite* | A stone that helps with forgiveness and healing old painful wounds. | |
| *Rose quartz* | The go-to stone for matters of healing the heart, certainly relevant in any discussion of painful losses. | |

# Crystals for Calm

## Correspondences for Calling In Calm

- *The color PALE BLUE*
- *The lower chakras*
- *The herb chamomile*

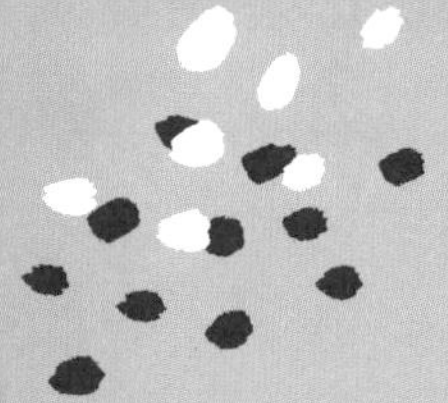

**Suggested practices:** *Bath rituals, meditation, visualization, stretching and medicinal movement*

One of the most common ways people work with crystals is to invite calm into their lives. Some crystals are energetic activators—stones that can amplify or electrify people, places, and things. However, there are a variety of other crystals that can act as soothing and calming agents. This is why crystals are often used in yoga studios and meditative spaces, and why crystal sound instruments are a good choice for meditative journeys.

To engage with a crystal in an appreciative and intentionally present manner can be very calming in and of itself. Crystals are beautiful, and with some of them, you can get lost in their facets, watching how the light reflects and shifts within them. To sit and examine a crystal can be an act of mindfulness—a practice of anchoring yourself fully in the felt experience of the moment.

Crystals have long been associated with spirituality and ritual, allowing them to serve as a visual prompt for mysticism and mystery. When decorating your spaces, you may want to use calming crystals in areas that you would like to have a soft and soothing vibe, such as the bedroom or living room. If you want to test for yourself how calming crystals work for you personally, try meditating twice—once with crystals and once without—then take note of your results!

## Bonus tip!

***Although not technically crystals, smooth rocks that have been collected from a calming place such as a beach or creek can also be incorporated into your "stone toolkit" for calm, particularly if you have a strong memory of peacefulness from the day you collected the stones or if you associate tranquillity with the location where you gathered them.***

## A Suggested Practice

Although it can feel as if calm is a million miles away when you are going through it, the truth is that, in many cases, calming down is easy once a person stops trying to fight their panic, fear, or restlessness and embraces the felt sense of the body, allowing those feelings and their corresponding physical symptoms to pass.

To start this process, turn to the breath. If you are in need of a bit of calm, take two palmstones or small tumbled stones that correspond to calm from the suggested list opposite. Make sure these crystals have been energetically cleared and are ready for use. Place one in each hand and sit in the lotus position if you are able to. Close your eyes as you hold your stones and take six to ten deep, cleansing breaths, focusing on the sensation of your breath and the feeling of the crystals in your palms. What texture do they have? What temperature are they?

Inhale deeply, imagining that the calming effect of the stones is seeping through your tender palms and into your entire body. Exhale for a slightly longer count than your inhale, imagining that any stress, tension, and worries are exiting your body with each breath. Afterward, sit with the calm that this practice will bring to your body for as long as you need.

# Suggested Crystals for Calm

| | | |
|---|---|---|
| *Agate* | A grounding and calming stone that stabilizes and soothes negative energies. | |
| *Blue lace agate* | A stone of peace and tranquillity that helps dispel bad feelings and stress. | |
| *Aquamarine* | A healing stone that promotes clarity and provides mental calm. | |
| *Howlite* | A calming stone that helps with sleep and neutralizing intense emotions. | |
| *Moonstone* | Provides support and healing, as well as dampening reactive emotions. | |

# Crystals for Self-Love and Acceptance

## Correspondences for Self-Love and Acceptance

- *The color PINK*
- *The heart chakra*
- *The flower rose*

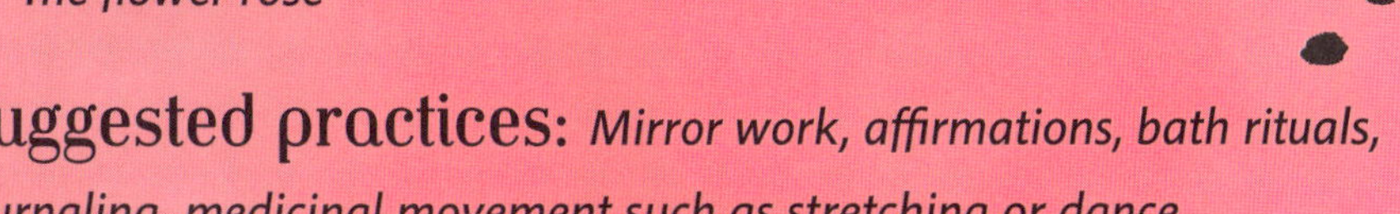

**Suggested practices:** *Mirror work, affirmations, bath rituals, journaling, medicinal movement such as stretching or dance*

Self-love and self-acceptance are the foundations upon which an authentic life is built. Far beyond just confidence or self-esteem, having acceptance and love for oneself is the foundation from which all manner of growth can take place. Despite the fact that it may seem in our best interests to love and accept ourselves, the truth is that reaching a place where this feels safe and easy can take a lot of inner work and energetic realignment. Just naturally accepting who we are in all our messy glory is unfortunately a skill that we do not seem to cultivate well in our society.

Part of the reason these things seem to be in such short supply is that we are subtly programmed by the larger culture to reject ourselves or see ourselves as not good enough. "Hot or not" headlines and pervasive media messages telling us—both subtly and not so subtly—all the ways we fall short can leave us second-guessing our worth. Then there are the regular interactions we have with others in our circle as we grow up, some of which may leave us with strange ideas about ourselves and our right to be authentically us. It is truly the work of a lifetime to reconnect with our worthiness and find self-acceptance!

From an energy healing standpoint, crystals that are heart openers and work with the Anahata, or heart chakra, are perfect for self-love practices. The vibration of these crystals is meant to help realign blockages and soothe a wounded heart. Although there are many rituals, practices, and techniques each of us can use to help us overcome the mindset and emotional issues associated with low self-esteem, crystals can be a wonderful and vibrant addition to our practices. For issues related to the heart chakra, it is often recommended to keep a heart-opening stone close to your chest. This can be easily accomplished with jewelry, such as a rose quartz necklace.

## A Suggested Practice

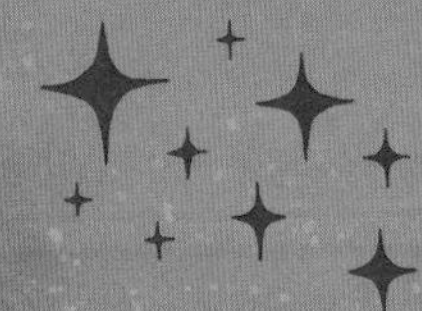

A simple way to use crystals for self-love and acceptance is to make a crystal elixir.* Crystal elixirs are waters that have been infused with the energy and vibrations of crystals. It is crucial to note that crystal elixirs are not always safe. Please refer to the section on crystal safety in this book and consult your crystal guides to determine whether your chosen stones are safe to use in this way. For this practice, I suggest rose quartz, as it is a great stone for self-love and also water-safe (for short periods of time).

To make an elixir, first cleanse a clear glass jar and fill it with fresh, pure water (spring water works well for this). Next, take your rose quartz and cleanse it both physically (removing any dust or debris) and energetically. Place the crystal in your jar, then add the water. Leave this mix out in moonlight for a few hours, then remove the crystal and strain the water through muslin or a fine sieve into a jar or bottle where you can store the water. You can add a few drops of this elixir to your drinking water for increased self-acceptance, or you can use the gem-infused water to wash your face or add it to your bath water for improved self-love.

** Make sure not to ingest ANY part of the crystal or any piece of broken crystal. Do not leave the crystal submerged in the water for too long, and make sure you use your elixir within a few days to a week.*

# Suggested Crystals for Self-Love and Acceptance

| | | |
|---|---|---|
| *Rose quartz* | The quintessential heart stone, rose quartz helps with the heart chakra energy center and provides a soothing, loving energy to those who work with it. | |
| *Agate* | Helps facilitate self-acceptance, providing a calming and supportive vibe for working through traumas and anxieties. | |
| *Malachite* | This is a protective stone that can allow for heart-centered transformation and acceptance of oneself beyond old wounds and traumas. | |
| *Amazonite* | A stone with the ability to balance energies and work with the heart center for self-love, helping to release old negative patterns and emotions. | |
| *Moonstone* | A soothing stone that can promote kindness and empathy toward oneself and others, providing peace and stability. | |

# Crystals and Confidence

## Correspondences for Confidence

- *The color RED, or other BOLD colors, particularly if they evoke feelings of strength for you*
- *The lower chakras, particularly the solar plexus*
- *The spice cinnamon*

**Suggested practices:** *Stretching and body posture awareness, mirror work, affirmations, journaling, creating*

Many people struggle with a lack of confidence, whether related to appearance, insecurities and body image, speaking their mind, or the courage to chase their dreams and the things they want in life. The truth is that we are often limited only by our perceptions of ourselves, and a lack of confidence can cause us to dig our heels into our "stuck-ness," becoming a self-fulfilling prophecy that gathers "evidence" for why we aren't good enough.

The good news is that confidence is a quality that can be learned and developed. And crystals can be a great companion to your confidence work, as their power and portability can give you a glittering confidence boost, even while on the go!

When it comes to confidence, discussions of vibrations and frequency are highly relevant. After all, confidence has its own frequency—a stable and grounded energy that radiates from a person. Many people assume confidence is primarily a mental process, which it undoubtedly is, but there is an energetic component that cannot be discounted. For confidence work, a person must delve into their own wounds and subconscious beliefs regarding how they conceptualize themselves, while also being able to hold the energy of confidence and self-trust, even in unfamiliar and unpleasant situations. Crystals can be a helpful addition to your inner work to overcome insecurity and banish self-doubt.

## A Suggested Practice

If you have a piece of crystal jewelry that corresponds to confidence (rose quartz is a fairly common one) or even just a portable tumbled stone, you can create a talisman for confidence that you can sit with at home while doing confidence work, and wear on your person while you are out and about.

Start by cleansing and clearing your stone or piece of jewelry using whichever method you choose, then program your item to serve as your confidence-boosting amulet. To do this, get a sense of what that confidence would look like in action. Would it be the ability not to shrink as you walk into a room or to speak up in difficult situations? It can be worthwhile to explore this by reflecting in a journal or notebook beforehand.

Cup your item in your hands, and state aloud your intention for the work you want it to do. As you hold your crystal or piece of jewelry, visualize the kind of confidence you are calling in and sense the vibration of the crystal realigning your energies to match your intention. It's important to hold this vision in your mind's eye while programming your crystal, until you can feel the emotions or sensations in your body.

After this programming, bring your crystal with you as an energetic anchor, or wear your piece of jewelry with the knowledge that its vibrations will be working on you as you move forward. Ask your stone to influence your field in a way that allows you to feel safe and stable in situations where you may need to take up space or advocate for yourself. When you carry it while you are out and about, pay attention to your body when situations arise where you are tempted to "dim" or energetically "restrict" yourself. If you are in a situation where you could use a quick confidence boost, take a moment to breathe intentionally, imagining that you are absorbing the strong vibrations from your confidence crystals.

# Suggested Crystals for Confidence

| | | |
|---|---|---|
| *Red chalcedony* | A stone that corresponds with strength and stability; works well for uniting body, mind, and spirit. | |
| *Citrine* | A powerhouse of a crystal that corresponds with confidence, creativity, and positivity. | |
| *Fluorite* | A protective stone with positive energy; helps with improving self-esteem and self-understanding. | |
| *Garnet* | A cleansing and strengthening stone that helps with releasing old mental and emotional baggage. | |
| *Rose quartz* | Once again, this heart stone can come in handy in matters related to self-love and opening the heart chakra. | |

# Crystals for Empowered Self-Expression

## Correspondences for Self-Expression

- *The color BLUE*
- *The throat chakra*
- *The herb peppermint*

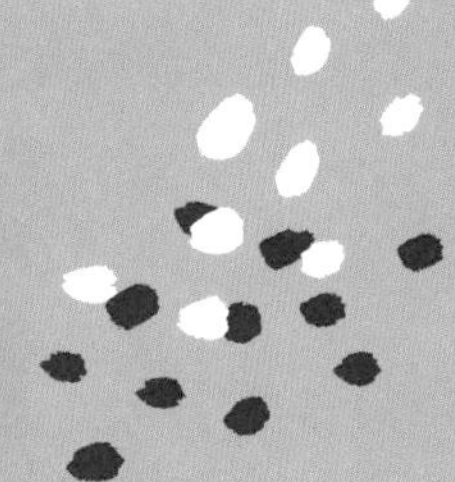

**Suggested practices:** *Affirmations, creating, singing or humming, dancing, journaling*

Issues with self-expression are closely linked to confidence and self-acceptance, but for our purposes we will focus on self-expression alone here. You may experience challenges with expressing the fullness of who you authentically are in terms of your appearance, the things you do with your time and your personality, or you may face difficulties when it comes to literally expressing yourself in the vocal or spoken sense.

In the case of authentic self-expression, there is often a great deal of programming that needs to be undone when it comes to how loudly and boldly you can amplify your magic. Although we, as a society, claim to support free self-expression for all, significant fallout can occur when a person really does express themselves freely. As a collective, many of us carry a deep feeling that it is somehow "naughty" to be our loudest, boldest selves, and we often experience situations where our self-expression is not well received by others.

Self-expression can include things like advocating for yourself, setting boundaries and speaking your mind. All of these can elicit strong feelings in others, but that should not be a barrier for you! Every person has the right to express themselves in a way that feels authentic and good. After all, we are only here for a limited time!

## A Suggested Practice

A wonderful way to use crystals for self-expression is to harness their energy while you practice expressing yourself aloud in the privacy of your own home, until you become more comfortable and confident doing so out in the big wide world. This is something you can practice until you build comfort on an energetic level. A fun way to use crystals is to play some lively music, gather some stones that promote self-expression (blue stones that correspond to the vishuddha, or throat chakra) and have a song and dance party!

Let loose and sing or vent out loud—the goal is to release your inhibitions without judging yourself or allowing your inner censor to shut you down. Feel free to dance wildly and give yourself permission to express yourself through your movements and voice in a way that isn't bogged down by self-consciousness or other concerns that keep you timid.

We all need some time to let loose, and when we give ourselves permission to experience what it's like to do so in a safe space, it helps us become stronger in other settings.

# Suggested Crystals for Self-Expression

| | | |
|---|---|---|
| *Lapis lazuli* | A throat chakra activating stone that works for self-expression, clarity, and harmony. | |
| *Clear quartz* | A multipurpose stone that amplifies energies and helps to align the energy centers of the body. | |
| *Iron pyrite* | This stone helps with confidence, energy, and tapping into personal potential. | |
| *Carnelian* | An invigorating stone that encourages strength, vitality, and clarity. | |
| *Amazonite* | A loving stone that helps to release fear and aids in clear communication. | |

# Crystals and Creativity

## Correspondences for Creativity

- *The color ORANGE*
- *The sacral chakra, crown, and third eye*
- *The herb lemon balm*

**Suggested practices:** *Vision boards, journaling, art, visualization practices, daydreaming*

Creativity is a sacred element of the human condition. Distinct from artistic ability, the capacity for creativity has allowed our species to thrive in a variety of ways. Sometimes, a lack of creativity can be felt in a big way—whether as a barrier to dreaming up novel solutions to problems or as a struggle with creative blocks of all kinds.

To live a creative life is our birthright as human beings. We are constantly generating new thoughts and ideas, and some among us have honed the ability to turn this tendency into art, living in offbeat yet fulfilling ways, and finding their authenticity by living boldly and freely. If you fear that you're not a creative person, I recommend looking at the wild and unlikely scenarios your anxiety has dreamt up! This is a good illustration of the fact that creativity is inherent to how we think and not synonymous with artistic ability.

Crystals can offer a great energetic boost to help remove creative blocks and barriers of all kinds! Aesthetically, they can act as a primer for appreciating the beauty and glory of nature. Energetically, stones that are meant to charge and activate us to be more creatively open can help us overcome self-doubt and limiting beliefs, allowing us to be inspired by ourselves and the world around us.

## A Suggested Practice

A crystal grid is a great way to invite creative energy into your world. Because crystal grids can be set up and activated to work over a period, they are a fantastic way to introduce some crystal-boosted creative vibes into your life. Creativity is not a thing that we sit down to "do" for specified chunks of time—it is a fundamental dimension of the human experience, and as such, inspiration can strike whenever, wherever! By setting up a grid, you are opening yourself up to these creative strikes in an ongoing way.

First set your intention. What does calling in creativity mean to you? Are you seeking increased motivation to create? A hope that inspiration will visit more often? Do you want to find the courage to live a bold, creative life? Getting clear on your intention will help you find success.

Next, choose your stones, including a center crystal and surrounding stones. There is a list of a few crystals that correspond to creativity opposite, but feel free to consult your crystal guidebooks or use the ones that work best for you. To make your grid, you can use any shape you choose, but if you have access to a Flower of Life or Metatron's Cube sacred geometry grid, these patterns correspond well to creation and the interconnected nature of all things. Make sure to activate your grid with the specifics of your intention in mind!

# Suggested Crystals for Creativity

| | | |
|---|---|---|
| *Kunzite* | This stone aids in self-expression and helps people connect inspiration to action. | |
| *Celestine* | A deeply spiritual stone that can help open creative channels and facilitate clarity of communication. | |
| *Orange Calcite* | A stone that aids in moving past fears and insecurities and helps bring ideas to life. | |
| *Carnelian* | Enhances clarity, creativity, energy, and motivation. | |
| *Citrine* | Stimulates creativity, self-expression, and abundance of all kinds. | |

# Crystals for Energy

## Correspondences for Energy

- *The colors RED, ORANGE, and YELLOW*
- *The solar plexus chakra*
- *The herb ashwagandha*

**Suggested practices:** *Dance, goal setting, breathwork, exercise, creating*

One common woe that brings people to crystal healing is a lack of energy. This could be the result of a specific physical ailment or perhaps a more general mental or energetic dip. Thanks to the activating and energizing potentials of certain crystals, they are often called upon when a person could use a little energy boost! When it comes to harnessing crystals for energy, it's important to define what it is you are trying to achieve. For some, it may be physical energy, leading them to work with stones that correspond to specific areas of the body or chakra points (particularly the *Manipura* or solar plexus). For others, this may be about motivation or finding their "spark." If you want to begin troubleshooting a lack of energy using crystals, the first step is to check in with your circumstances and ask yourself, *"What exactly is it that I need?"*

As with any physical issue, a lack of energy should always be taken seriously in case there is a medical cause. Crystals are a fantastic way to take our wellness into our own hands, but as we've noted, they alone are not enough to solve many of our problems. The beauty of energy work, crystals and other psychospiritual modalities is that they can serve as parts of a comprehensive personal wellness plan. Just as you typically would not paint a vibrant and compelling picture with just one color, you shouldn't rely on a single method for healing; instead, ensure you diversify and explore as many avenues to healing and wellness as possible!

## A Suggested Practice

Sit in a space with your energizing crystals nearby. If you have the space and enough crystals to do so, create a circle large enough for you to sit inside. Make sure your crystals have been cleansed and programmed for this purpose. To do this, you must clarify your intention based on what you are trying to accomplish—what does a boost in energy mean for you?

Sit down and begin to take deep, intentional breaths. As you breathe in, visualize the activating vibration of the crystals rising like a mist into your body. As you exhale, imagine expelling all the dull, stagnant energies that you are trying to revitalize. Keep doing these cycles of breath until you feel a rush in your physical body. Then take a moment to sit with that feeling to anchor it in.

If it helps, you can follow this exercise by carrying your crystals around with you in a pocket or charm bag. This works best if you have small, tumbled stones that are hard enough that they are not at high risk of chipping or breaking.

# Suggested Crystals for Energy and Motivation

| | | |
|---|---|---|
| *Yellow jasper* | A stimulating stone that can boost positive energy. | |
| *Unakite* | A visionary stone of transformation that stimulates healing. | |
| *Carnelian* | This energizing stone aids in increased positive energy and clarity. | |
| *Garnet* | A power stone that facilitates the stimulation of positive energies in the body and mind. | |
| *Fluorite* | A cleansing stone that can facilitate organization and clarity, allowing thoughts to become actions. | |

# Crystals and Connecting to Intuition and the Higher Self

## Correspondences for Intuition

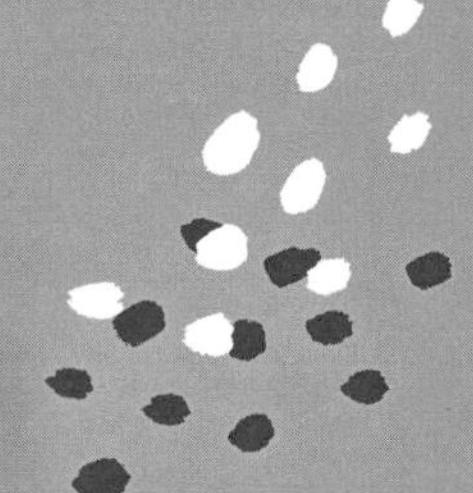

- *The colors INDIGO, PURPLE, and SILVER*
- *The third eye and crown chakras*
- *The tree or shrub juniper*

**Suggested practices:** *Bath rituals, meditation, creating, divination practices, dreamwork*

Intuition is a power that we all possess, but not one that we are typically taught how to use. You may have experienced it before in your life—a gut feeling that helped you make a decision, or a circumstance where you had the undeniable sense that something was amiss. This may have been your intuition in action—your inner guidance that can act as a compass and navigation system.

When it comes to intuition, the best way to forge a connection is to understand its language—how it communicates with you. For some, intuition manifests as an inner voice. For others, it may be a "gut" feeling or bodily sensation. There is no one right way that intuition calls to us. It is part of your inner operating system, and as such, you will be the best authority on how it speaks to you and how to develop it.

Intuition typically corresponds to the third eye and crown and the colors indigo, purple, and silver. The topic of intuition is often clustered with other practices such as dreamwork, divination, connecting to the higher self or spirit guides, and more.

No conversation about connecting to your intuition would be complete without acknowledging that listening to your inner voice does not always mean getting things right. Sometimes our intuition may lead us to unexpected places that can leave us second guessing ourselves. It can be helpful to zoom out and understand that the "right" way for us in any given situation is not always the way we had imagined beforehand. Be grounded, but allow your intuition to be more creative and surprising than you may have prepared for.

## A Suggested Practice

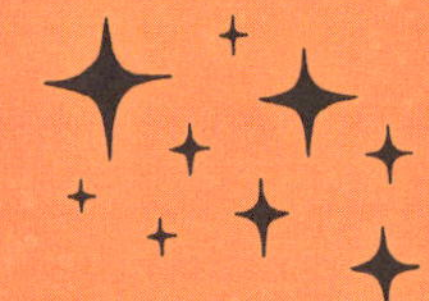

One way to connect with your intuition using crystals is through dreaming or meditation. Take your crystals (see the list opposite for suggestions) and cleanse and programme them to help activate your third eye and connect to your intuition. Place your crystals by your bedside,* with the intention of activating your connection to your intuition and inner guidance. This can occur through dreams or by meditating beside the crystals. You may even try placing a crystal on the third eye area of your forehead, and then engage in meditation to see what happens.

It's important to make a note of what comes up for you, as this can form the foundation of your budding relationship with your intuition. You can write down your reflections in a dream or meditation journal. Make sure you remain open minded and take the time to charge and cleanse your crystals periodically.

**You can find creative ways to do this that are also aesthetically pleasing, for example, creating a crystal grid by your bedside or making a small dream/meditation altar.*

# Suggested Crystals for Connecting to Intuition

| | |
|---|---|
| Labradorite | A highly psychic stone that is also protective. Labradorite is often used to connect with the higher psychic realms.  |
| Fluorite | A cleansing stone that can help shield and protect a person on the psychic level.  |
| Sodalite | Helps to clear the mind and enhance the connection with intuition and higher guidance.  |
| Amethyst | Helps to increase mental focus and clarity; aids in facilitating a strong link between the physical, mental, and the spiritual.  |
| Lapis Lazuli | A third eye stone that can help unlock personal power and enhance connection to intuition and the Divine.  |

# Crystals for Abundance

## Correspondences for Abundance

- *The color GREEN*
- *The root chakra*
- *The herb basil*

**Suggested practices:** *Cleansing your spaces, goal setting, vision boards, journaling, giving back*

For better or worse, crystals are typically associated with New Age movements, so the crystal conversation is often entwined with topics like manifestation, the Law of Attraction, and a variety of other psychospiritual systems that aim to help with the more earthly dimensions of reality—things like material wealth and abundance.

The reality is that although money cannot buy happiness, a certain amount of freedom and ease can come when a person is not stuck in financial or energetic survival mode. For this reason, the act of manifesting abundance or wealth can be reframed as an act of self-care. This isn't the same perspective as those "think positive and get a Ferrari" kinds of belief systems. This is more about being energetically open to opportunity, finding ladders out of scarcity, and dramatically rethinking what wellness encompasses in a practical sense.

There is a tendency to see manifesting wealth as a naughty or superficial act, usually due to our beliefs surrounding the virtues of both being wealthy and experiencing scarcity. There are many examples in stories and the media where we are fed the concept that having money is a dirty thing, while being unconcerned about wealth is seen as pure and virtuous.

I mention these things because they are the subconscious beliefs that undermine our ability to manifest or attract wealth, or as I prefer to conceptualize it, resources. No amount of work with crystals can counteract the deep subconscious beliefs that cause us to actively repel that which we claim to want. The good news is that crystals can be a potent ally in helping us realign our beliefs and the vibration of judgemental scarcity when doing this work!

## A Suggested Practice

Create an abundance altar in a space that you consider the "heart" of your home. For some, this might be a living room or kitchen. If you share your home with others, you may want to use your bedroom, as this would be in essence the heart of your space.

An altar is simply a ritual space. It doesn't have to be big or complicated, so don't overthink it! On your altar, you may want to collect items that symbolize abundance or wealth to you, such as coins, flowers, or anything else that fits. Take some crystals that correspond with wealth and plenitude (see the suggested list opposite), cleanse and charge them for the purpose of calling in abundance, and arrange them on your altar.

To enhance this practice, write down an affirmation or statement of intent in the active tense (I am, I will, etc.) that clearly states your goals around what you are looking to call in. Place this on your altar underneath your crystals. Make sure to tend to your altar, refreshing the charge of your crystals and ensuring they stay energetically activated.

# Suggested Crystals for Abundance

| | | |
|---|---|---|
| *Citrine* | For abundance and positive energy. This is a great stone for manifesting and attracting success. |  |
| *Aventurine* | For success and prosperity. This stone can bring abundance and increase creativity. |  |
| *Turquoise* | A spiritual stone that calls in positive energy and abundance. | 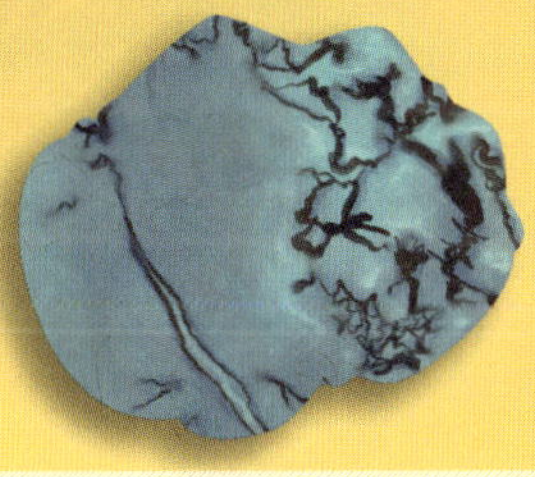 |
| *Iron pyrite* | An invigorating stone that activates positive potential and prosperity. |  |
| *Moss agate* | A harmonious stone that can aid in problem solving and manifesting solutions. |  |

# Your Crystal Care Plan

By now, you're hopefully feeling confident about using crystals in your wellness and self-care routines. As we've covered throughout this book, there are many ways to use crystals to enhance your life, whether by targeting specific issues or simply experimenting with these beautiful and vibrant stones.

This is the part where you can establish a crystal care plan for yourself moving forward!

As you probably noticed in this last part of the book, there are a variety of crystals that serve multiple purposes. Clear quartz, rose quartz, and amethyst are good examples of easily available multipurpose crystals that can act on a variety of intentions. When building your crystal collection, you may want to begin by using some of these more common, affordable, and versatile stones. The following is a list to get you started, but feel free to follow your intuition and personal needs!

When beginning to work with crystals, you may want to keep a crystal diary or journal in which you can track the crystals you have used and the ways you have used them, keeping track of the results to develop the best care plan that works for you!

As you move forward, be sure to cultivate a relationship with your stones that is open-minded, respectful, and honest. Because ultimately, your intention for working with them is enhanced personal wellness and self-care—the very same things they have been used for throughout the history of humanity!

# Glossary

**Amorphous solid**—A rock that does not have a crystalline structure

**Amplifier**—A device that increases signal, energy, or current

**Astrology**—The study of the planets and stars and their influence on human behavior

**Chakras**—Seven energy points across the body

**Crystalline**—Having the structure of a crystal

**Crystal lattice**—The geometric arrangement of atoms, molecules, or ions within crystals

**Divination**—The art of seeing the future

**Electromagnetic**—Relating to the force between electric and magnetic fields

**Elemental**—Relating to the elements

**Elixir**—A liquid concoction

**Ethical**—Morally right

**Geode**—A crystal-filled hole in a rock

**Geometric**—Consisting of or relating to shapes

**Lapidary**—Relating to the practice or art of shaping stones, gems, and minerals through cutting, polishing, or engraving

**Magma**—Liquefied rock from under Earth's crust

**Manifestation**—The act of making something real, often through belief

**Metaphysical**—Relating to existence and reality

**New Age**—A movement that explores alternatives to traditional Western religion and spirituality

**Placebo**—A medical treatment or substance with no medical components, often used as a control in experiments

**Polarization**—The division of opposing things, like two opposing magnets

**Pseudoscience**—Practices, beliefs, and claims that are mistakenly thought to be based on science

**Pyroelectricity**—Electricity generated by some crystals when heated or cooled

**Quartz**—A very hard crystal consisting of silica

**Realm**—A domain or sphere that exists or is thought to exist

**Ritual**—Any action that is performed at a certain time or in a certain way

**Scrying**—A form of divination using a crystal ball

**Shamanistic**—Relating to shamanism, a spiritual practice that deals with the spiritual realms

**Somatic shift**—A physical change that can be felt within the body

**Synthetic**—Made by humans using a chemical process

**Tektite**—A glass object formed from meteorites that have fallen to Earth

**Tower**—A crystal that can stand alone on a flat base, with a tall, pointed shaft